THIS BOOK BELONGS TO

The Library of

....

....

Did you like my book? I pondered it severely before releasing this book. Although the response has been overwhelming, it is always pleasing to see, read or hear a new comment. Thank you for reading this and I would love to hear your honest opinion about it. Furthermore, many people are searching for a unique book, and your feedback will help me gather the right books for my reading audience.

Thanks!

Table of Contents

SUMMARY

The Art of Mosaic Crochet: The Art of Mosaic Crochet is a fascinating and intricate form of crochet that combines the traditional techniques of crochet with the art of mosaic design. This unique style of crochet allows for the creation of stunning and complex patterns that resemble the look of mosaic tiles.

Mosaic crochet is achieved by using two or more colors of yarn and working in a combination of single crochet stitches and slip stitches. The slip stitches are used to create the mosaic effect, as they are worked over the stitches of the previous row, creating a raised texture that mimics the appearance of mosaic tiles.

One of the key aspects of mosaic crochet is the use of color. By strategically placing different colors of yarn, intricate patterns and designs can be created. The contrast between the colors adds depth and dimension to the finished piece, making it visually striking and eye-catching.

The technique of mosaic crochet may seem complex at first, but with practice and patience, it can be mastered. There are various resources available, such as books, online tutorials, and workshops, that can help beginners learn the basics and develop their skills in this art form.

One of the advantages of mosaic crochet is its versatility. It can be used to create a wide range of items, from blankets and scarves to bags and home decor. The possibilities are endless, and the only limit is one's imagination.

In addition to its aesthetic appeal, mosaic crochet also offers a sense of relaxation and mindfulness. The repetitive nature of the stitches can be soothing and meditative, allowing the crocheter to enter a state of flow and focus. It can be a wonderful way to unwind and de-stress after a long day.

The Art of Mosaic Crochet is not only a creative outlet but also a form of self-expression. Each piece created is unique and reflects the individuality and style of the crocheter. It allows for personalization and customization, making it a truly personal art form.

Whether you are a seasoned crocheter looking to expand your skills or a beginner eager to learn a new technique, the Art of Mosaic Crochet offers a world of possibilities. With its intricate patterns, vibrant colors, and therapeutic benefits, it is a truly captivating and rewarding art form to explore. So grab your crochet hook and yarn, and let your creativity soar with the Art of Mosaic Crochet.

Modern Interpretations of Ancient Geometric Patterns in Mosaic Crochet: Modern interpretations of ancient geometric patterns in mosaic crochet have become increasingly popular in recent years. This unique form of crochet combines the traditional technique of creating intricate patterns with the use of bold and vibrant colors, resulting in visually stunning and contemporary designs.

Mosaic crochet itself is a technique that involves working with two or more colors in a single row or round, creating a mosaic-like effect. This technique allows crocheters to create intricate geometric patterns that resemble the ancient mosaic art found in various cultures throughout history.

One of the reasons why modern interpretations of ancient geometric patterns in mosaic crochet have gained so much popularity is the versatility of this technique. Crocheters can create a wide range of designs, from simple and minimalist patterns to more complex and intricate ones. This allows for endless possibilities and allows crocheters to express their creativity and personal style.

Another reason for the popularity of modern interpretations of ancient geometric patterns in mosaic crochet is the ability to incorporate different color combinations. Crocheters can experiment with various color schemes, from monochromatic and neutral tones to bold and contrasting hues. This adds depth and dimension to the patterns, making them visually striking and eye-catching.

Furthermore, modern interpretations of ancient geometric patterns in mosaic crochet have also become popular due to the accessibility of the technique. With the availability of online tutorials, patterns, and resources, crocheters of all skill levels can easily learn and master this technique. This has led to a growing community of mosaic crochet enthusiasts who share their creations and inspire others to explore this unique form of crochet.

In addition to its aesthetic appeal, modern interpretations of ancient geometric patterns in mosaic crochet also have practical benefits. The use of bold and contrasting colors can help highlight specific areas of a design, creating a focal point or emphasizing certain elements. This can be particularly useful when creating home decor items such as blankets, pillows, or wall hangings.

Overall, modern interpretations of ancient geometric patterns in mosaic crochet offer a fresh and contemporary take on a traditional craft. The combination of intricate patterns, vibrant colors, and the versatility of the technique make mosaic crochet a captivating and rewarding form of artistic expression. Whether you are a seasoned crocheter or a beginner, exploring this technique can open up a world of possibilities and allow you to create unique and visually stunning pieces that pay homage to the ancient art of mosaics.

What is Mosaic Crochet?

Mosaic crochet is a unique crochet technique that involves creating intricate and visually stunning patterns using a combination of different colored yarns. It is a method that allows crocheters to create complex designs and motifs by working with multiple colors in a single row or round.

The term "mosaic" refers to the way the colors are combined to create the pattern. Instead of changing colors within a row or round, mosaic crochet uses a combination of stitches and color placement to achieve the desired design. This technique typically involves working with two or more colors at a time, with one color being used for the main body of the project and the other colors used for the design elements.

One of the key features of mosaic crochet is the use of special stitches, such as the slip stitch and the single crochet, to create the mosaic effect. These stitches are used to create a textured fabric that resembles a mosaic tile pattern. By working these stitches in a specific sequence and following a chart or pattern, crocheters can create intricate and detailed designs that resemble traditional mosaic artwork.

Mosaic crochet offers a wide range of design possibilities, as crocheters can create geometric shapes, floral motifs, and even realistic images using this technique. The use of different colors and stitch combinations allows for endless creativity and customization. Additionally, mosaic crochet can be used to create a variety of projects, including blankets, scarves, hats, and even garments.

While mosaic crochet may seem complex and intimidating at first, it is a technique that can be learned and mastered with practice. There are many resources available, including books, online tutorials, and workshops, that can help beginners get started and improve their skills. With time and patience, crocheters can develop their own unique style and create beautiful mosaic crochet projects.

In conclusion, mosaic crochet is a captivating and versatile technique that allows crocheters to create intricate and visually stunning patterns using a combination of different colored yarns. With its endless design possibilities and the ability to create unique and personalized projects, mosaic crochet is a technique that is sure to inspire and delight crocheters of all skill levels.

The Beauty of Geometric Designs in Mosaic Crochet: Mosaic crochet is a technique that combines the art of crochet with the beauty of geometric designs. It involves using multiple colors of yarn to create intricate patterns and shapes, resulting in stunning and visually appealing pieces of art.

One of the most captivating aspects of mosaic crochet is the way it allows for the creation of complex geometric designs. By using different combinations of stitches and colors, crocheters can produce patterns that resemble intricate mosaics or tessellations. These designs often feature repeating motifs, such as squares, triangles, or hexagons, which are arranged in a symmetrical and visually pleasing manner.

The beauty of geometric designs in mosaic crochet lies in their ability to create a sense of order and harmony. The precise placement of stitches and colors creates a structured and balanced composition, which is both visually striking and aesthetically pleasing. The repetition of geometric shapes adds a sense of rhythm and flow to the design, further enhancing its appeal.

Another fascinating aspect of mosaic crochet is the way it allows for the exploration of color combinations. Crocheters can experiment with different hues and shades, creating unique and vibrant patterns. The use of contrasting colors can create a bold and eye-catching effect, while the use of subtle gradients can produce a more subtle and sophisticated look. The possibilities are endless, and each color choice can dramatically alter the overall appearance of the design.

In addition to their visual appeal, geometric designs in mosaic crochet also offer a sense of challenge and accomplishment for crocheters. The intricate patterns require careful attention to detail and precision in stitch placement. This level of complexity can be both rewarding and satisfying for those who enjoy a more advanced crochet technique.

Furthermore, mosaic crochet designs can be applied to a wide range of projects, from blankets and scarves to home decor items and clothing. The versatility of this technique allows crocheters to incorporate geometric designs into their creations in various ways, adding a touch of elegance and sophistication to their finished pieces.

In conclusion, the beauty of geometric designs in mosaic crochet lies in their ability to create visually stunning and harmonious compositions. The precise placement of stitches and colors, along with the exploration of different color combinations, results in intricate and captivating patterns. The challenge and versatility of this technique make it a favorite among crochet enthusiasts, allowing them to create unique and impressive pieces of art. Whether you are a beginner or an experienced crocheter, exploring the world of mosaic crochet and its geometric designs is sure to inspire and delight.

Tools and Materials Overview of Mosaic Crochet: Mosaic crochet is a technique that combines the art of crochet with the visual appeal of mosaic patterns. It involves creating intricate designs using two or more colors of yarn, resulting in a stunning and textured finished product. To successfully create mosaic crochet projects, you will need a variety of tools and materials.

First and foremost, you will need crochet hooks. The size of the hook you choose will depend on the weight of the yarn you are using and the desired tension of your stitches. It is recommended to have a range of hook sizes available, as different projects may require different hook sizes to achieve the desired gauge.

Next, you will need yarn. Mosaic crochet typically involves using two or more colors of yarn to create the mosaic patterns. It is important to choose yarns that have good color contrast, as this will enhance the visual impact of the design. You can opt for any type of yarn, such as acrylic, cotton, or wool, depending on your personal preference and the intended use of the finished project.

In addition to crochet hooks and yarn, you will also need a few other tools to aid in the mosaic crochet process. Stitch markers are essential for keeping track of pattern repeats and color changes. These can be simple plastic rings or clips that can be easily attached and removed from your work.

A tapestry needle is another important tool for mosaic crochet. This needle is used for weaving in loose ends and tidying up the finished project. It is recommended to choose a tapestry needle with a large eye, as this will make it easier to thread the yarn through.

Finally, you may also want to invest in a blocking mat and pins. Blocking is the process of shaping and stretching your finished crochet project to ensure that it lays flat and the stitches are even. A blocking mat provides a stable surface for blocking, while pins are used to secure the project in place as it dries.

Overall, mosaic crochet is a beautiful and intricate technique that requires a range of tools and materials. By having the right crochet hooks, yarn, stitch markers, tapestry needle, and blocking mat, you will be well-equipped to create stunning mosaic crochet projects. So gather your supplies and get ready to embark on a creative journey filled with color and texture!

Understanding Mosaic Crochet Terminology: Mosaic crochet is a popular technique that involves creating intricate and visually stunning patterns using a combination of basic crochet stitches. However, understanding the terminology associated with mosaic crochet can be a bit overwhelming for beginners. In this article, we will delve into the various terms used in mosaic crochet and provide a detailed explanation of each.

1. Mosaic Crochet: Mosaic crochet is a technique that involves creating patterns using two or more colors of yarn. It typically involves working with two rows of stitches at a time, with one row being worked in the main color and the other row being worked in the contrasting color. The contrasting color is used to create the mosaic effect, where the stitches of the main color are partially covered by the contrasting color.

2. Main Color (MC): The main color refers to the color of yarn that forms the base of the pattern. It is the color that is predominantly visible in the finished project.

3. Contrasting Color (CC): The contrasting color is the color of yarn that is used to create the mosaic effect. It is typically a color that contrasts with the main color, making the pattern more visually appealing.

4. Mosaic Chart: A mosaic chart is a visual representation of the pattern that you will be crocheting. It consists of a grid with symbols or colors representing the different stitches and colors used in the pattern. Each square on the chart corresponds to a stitch in the pattern.

5. Mosaic Stitch: A mosaic stitch refers to the combination of stitches used to create the mosaic effect. It typically involves working a combination of single crochet (sc) and chain (ch) stitches in the main color, while using slip stitches (sl st) in the contrasting color to cover certain stitches.

6. Mosaic Pattern: A mosaic pattern is a specific design or motif that is created using the mosaic crochet technique. It can be a simple geometric pattern or a more complex image or picture.

7. Mosaic Repeat: A mosaic repeat refers to a specific sequence of stitches and color changes that is repeated throughout the pattern. It is usually indicated in the pattern instructions and helps to create the overall mosaic effect.

8. Mosaic Border: A mosaic border is a decorative edge that is added to the finished project to give it a polished and finished look. It can be a simple single crochet border or a more intricate pattern that complements the mosaic design.

Essential Stitches and Techniques of Mosaic Crochet: The Essential Stitches and Techniques of Mosaic Crochet is a comprehensive guide that delves into the intricate art of mosaic crochet. This technique combines the beauty of traditional crochet with the visual appeal of mosaic patterns, resulting in stunning and unique designs.

The book begins with an introduction to the history and origins of mosaic crochet, providing readers with a deeper understanding of its cultural significance. It then moves on to explain the basic stitches and techniques used in this style of crochet, ensuring that even beginners can follow along and create their own mosaic crochet projects.

One of the key features of this book is its detailed instructions and step-by-step tutorials. Each stitch and technique is explained in a clear and concise manner, accompanied by full-color photographs and diagrams. This allows readers to easily visualize and understand the process, making it easier to replicate the stitches and techniques in their own projects.

In addition to the basic stitches, the book also covers more advanced techniques such as color changes, pattern repeats, and shaping. These techniques are essential for creating intricate and complex mosaic crochet designs, and the book provides ample guidance and examples to help readers master them.

The book also includes a variety of mosaic crochet patterns, ranging from simple and beginner-friendly designs to more intricate and challenging projects. Each pattern is accompanied by detailed instructions, stitch charts, and color charts, making it easy for readers to follow along and create their own beautiful mosaic crochet pieces.

Furthermore, the book offers tips and tricks for troubleshooting common issues that may arise during the mosaic crochet process. Whether it's dealing with tension problems, fixing mistakes, or understanding pattern instructions, the book provides valuable insights and solutions to help readers overcome any obstacles they may encounter.

Overall, the Essential Stitches and Techniques of Mosaic Crochet is a must-have resource for anyone interested in exploring the world of mosaic crochet. With its comprehensive instructions, detailed tutorials, and inspiring patterns, this book is sure to inspire and empower crocheters of all skill levels to create their own stunning mosaic crochet masterpieces.

Reading Mosaic Crochet Charts: Reading Mosaic Crochet Charts is a skill that can greatly enhance your crochet abilities and open up a whole new world of design possibilities. Mosaic crochet is a technique that involves using two or more colors of yarn to create intricate patterns and designs. The charts used in mosaic crochet are visual representations of the pattern, with each square or symbol representing a specific stitch or color change.

To effectively read mosaic crochet charts, it is important to understand the symbols and their corresponding stitches. Each symbol on the chart represents a specific stitch, such as a single crochet, double crochet, or chain stitch. By familiarizing yourself with these symbols, you can easily follow the chart and create the desired pattern.

One of the key aspects of reading mosaic crochet charts is understanding color changes. In mosaic crochet, different colors are used to create the pattern. The chart will indicate when and where to change colors, allowing you to create intricate designs and motifs. By following the color changes on the chart, you can create beautiful and complex patterns that are sure to impress.

Another important aspect of reading mosaic crochet charts is understanding the repeat sections. Many mosaic crochet patterns have repeat sections, where a specific sequence of stitches or color changes is repeated multiple times. By identifying these repeat sections on the chart, you can save time and easily follow the pattern without constantly referring back to the chart.

Reading mosaic crochet charts also requires attention to detail. Each square or symbol on the chart represents a specific stitch or color change, and it is important to accurately follow these instructions to achieve the desired pattern. Paying close attention to the chart and double-checking your work can help ensure that your finished project matches the intended design.

In addition to understanding the symbols, color changes, repeat sections, and attention to detail, it is also helpful to have a basic understanding of crochet terminology and techniques. This will allow you to easily interpret the chart and understand the instructions provided.

Overall, reading mosaic crochet charts is a valuable skill that can greatly enhance your crochet abilities. By understanding the symbols, color changes, repeat sections, and paying attention to detail, you can confidently follow mosaic crochet patterns and create stunning designs. So, grab your crochet hook, some colorful yarn, and start exploring the world of mosaic crochet!

Selecting Color Palettes for Geometric Designs of Mosaic Crochet: When it comes to selecting color palettes for geometric designs in mosaic crochet, there are several factors to consider in order to achieve a visually appealing and harmonious result. Mosaic crochet is a technique that involves creating intricate patterns using two or more colors, typically in a grid-like structure. The choice of colors plays a crucial role in bringing out the desired geometric shapes and enhancing the overall aesthetic of the design.

One important aspect to consider when selecting color palettes for mosaic crochet is the intended mood or theme of the design. Different color combinations can evoke different emotions and create different atmospheres. For example, a vibrant and bold color palette with contrasting hues can create a lively and energetic design, while a more muted and monochromatic palette can give a design a more sophisticated and calming feel. It is important to have a clear vision of the desired mood or theme before selecting the colors.

Another factor to consider is the level of contrast between the colors. In mosaic crochet, contrast is key to creating well-defined geometric shapes. High contrast between the colors helps to make the individual shapes stand out and adds depth to the design. This can be achieved by selecting colors that are on opposite ends of the color spectrum, such as pairing a dark color with a light color or a warm color with a cool color. Experimenting with different levels of contrast can help determine the most visually appealing combination for the specific design.

Additionally, considering the color theory can be helpful in selecting color palettes for mosaic crochet. Color theory is the study of how colors interact with each other and how they can be combined to create pleasing compositions. Understanding concepts such as complementary colors (colors that are opposite each other on the color wheel), analogous colors (colors that are adjacent to each other on the color wheel), and color harmonies (combinations of colors that are aesthetically pleasing) can provide guidance in selecting colors that work well together in a geometric design.

Furthermore, taking inspiration from nature, art, or other sources can be a great starting point for selecting color palettes. Observing the colors found in natural landscapes, flowers, or artwork can provide inspiration and ideas for color combinations that can be translated into mosaic crochet designs. Looking at photographs, paintings, or even fashion magazines can help to identify color palettes that are visually appealing and can be adapted to the geometric shapes of mosaic crochet.

The Role of Contrast in Mosaic Patterns of Mosaic Crochet: Contrast plays a crucial role in the creation of mosaic patterns in mosaic crochet. Mosaic crochet is a technique that involves using two or more colors of yarn to create intricate and visually stunning designs. The use of contrasting colors is essential in order to achieve the desired effect and make the patterns stand out.

One of the main reasons why contrast is important in mosaic crochet is that it helps to define the different elements of the pattern. By using contrasting colors, the individual stitches and shapes become more distinct and easily recognizable. This is particularly important when working with complex designs that involve multiple colors and intricate details. Without contrast, the pattern may appear muddled and the different elements may blend together, making it difficult to discern the intended design.

Contrast also adds depth and dimension to mosaic crochet patterns. By using light and dark shades of the same color or contrasting colors, the pattern can create the illusion of depth and make it appear three-dimensional. This adds visual interest and makes the pattern more visually appealing.

Furthermore, contrast can be used strategically to highlight specific areas or elements of the pattern. By using a high contrast color for certain stitches or sections, those areas can be emphasized and draw the viewer's attention. This can be particularly effective when creating focal points or adding emphasis to certain parts of the design.

In addition to enhancing the visual appeal of the pattern, contrast also plays a practical role in mosaic crochet. It can help to differentiate between different stitches or techniques used in the pattern. For example, using a contrasting color for a specific stitch or technique can make it easier to identify and follow the instructions. This is especially useful for beginners or those who are new to mosaic crochet.

When choosing colors for mosaic crochet, it is important to consider the level of contrast between the colors. High contrast colors, such as black and white or complementary colors, create a bold and striking effect. On the other hand, low contrast colors, such as shades of the same color, create a more subtle and harmonious look. The choice of contrast depends on the desired outcome and the overall aesthetic of the pattern.

In conclusion, contrast plays a vital role in mosaic crochet patterns. It helps to define the different elements of the design, adds depth and dimension, highlights specific areas, and aids in the practicality of following the pattern. By carefully selecting and using contrasting colors, mosaic crochet enthusiasts can create stunning and visually captivating designs.

Experimenting with Color Changes of Mosaic Crochet: In recent years, there has been a growing trend in the world of crochet known as mosaic crochet. This technique involves creating intricate patterns and designs using a combination of different colored yarns. One of the most fascinating aspects of mosaic crochet is the ability to experiment with color changes, which can dramatically alter the overall look and feel of a project.

Color changes in mosaic crochet can be done in a variety of ways. One common method is to use multiple colors of yarn in a single row or round, creating a striped effect. This can be achieved by simply switching colors at the beginning or end of each row, or by carrying the unused yarn along the back of the work. By strategically placing the color changes, you can create bold, eye-catching designs that are sure to impress.

Another technique for experimenting with color changes in mosaic crochet is to use different shades of the same color. This can create a subtle gradient effect, where the colors blend seamlessly into one another. By using lighter and darker shades of the same color, you can add depth and dimension to your project, making it appear more three-dimensional.

In addition to using different colors and shades, you can also experiment with the placement of color changes in mosaic crochet. For example, you can create a checkerboard pattern by alternating between two colors in a grid-like formation. This can be done by working a row or round in one color, then switching to the second color for the next row or round, and so on. By varying the size and shape of the checkerboard squares, you can create a wide range of unique and visually appealing designs.

Furthermore, you can also experiment with the frequency of color changes in mosaic crochet. For a more subtle look, you can use fewer color changes, allowing the main color to dominate the design. On the other hand, if you want a more vibrant and dynamic project, you can incorporate frequent color changes, creating a mosaic effect that is full of energy and movement.

Overall, experimenting with color changes in mosaic crochet opens up a world of creative possibilities. Whether you choose to use multiple colors, different shades of the same color, or play around with the placement and frequency of color changes, the end result is sure to be a stunning and unique piece of crochet art. So why not grab your crochet hook and some colorful yarn, and start exploring the endless potential of mosaic crochet today?

Introducing Textures into Mosaic Crochet: Mosaic crochet is a technique that combines colorwork and texture to create stunning and intricate designs. Traditionally, mosaic crochet patterns are created using only different colors of yarn to form geometric shapes and patterns. However, with the introduction of textures into mosaic crochet, the possibilities for creating unique and visually appealing projects have expanded.

Textures can be added to mosaic crochet in a variety of ways. One common method is to use different stitches to create raised or textured areas within the design. For example, you can use front post double crochet stitches to create a ribbed effect or popcorn stitches to add a three-dimensional texture. By incorporating these textured stitches strategically within the mosaic pattern, you can create a visually interesting and dynamic design.

Another way to introduce textures into mosaic crochet is by using different types of yarn. By selecting yarns with varying thicknesses or textures, you can create a contrast in the overall look and feel of the project. For instance, using a chunky yarn for certain sections of the design can create a bold and textured effect, while using a finer yarn for other sections can add a delicate and intricate touch.

Additionally, you can experiment with different stitch combinations to create unique textures in your mosaic crochet projects. By combining different stitches, such as bobbles, cables, or clusters, you can create a wide range of textures and patterns within your design. This allows you to add depth and dimension to your mosaic crochet projects, making them visually captivating and engaging.

Introducing textures into mosaic crochet not only enhances the visual appeal of the projects but also adds a tactile element. The textured areas can create a more interesting and interactive experience for the viewer or wearer of the finished piece. Whether it's a cozy blanket, a stylish scarf, or a decorative wall hanging, the addition of textures can elevate the overall look and feel of the project.

In conclusion, incorporating textures into mosaic crochet opens up a world of possibilities for creating unique and visually stunning designs. By using different stitches, yarns, and stitch combinations, you can add depth, dimension, and tactile interest to your projects. Whether you're a beginner or an experienced crocheter, experimenting with textures in mosaic crochet can take your creations to the next level and allow you to express your creativity in new and exciting ways.

Working with Overlay Mosaic Crochet: Working with Overlay Mosaic Crochet is a fascinating and intricate technique that allows you to create stunning and visually appealing designs in your crochet projects. This technique involves working with multiple colors and overlaying stitches to create a mosaic-like effect.

To begin with, you will need to choose your colors and create a chart or pattern for your design. This can be done by either following an existing pattern or creating your own. The chart will serve as a guide for where to place each color and stitch in your project.

Once you have your chart ready, you can start working on your project. Overlay Mosaic Crochet typically involves working in rows or rounds, depending on the pattern. You will need to follow the chart and use different colors of yarn to create the desired design.

The key to achieving the mosaic effect is to overlay stitches on top of each other. This is done by working stitches in one color and then working stitches in another color on top of them. The stitches in the bottom layer will be partially covered by the stitches in the top layer, creating a layered and textured look.

One important thing to keep in mind when working with Overlay Mosaic Crochet is tension. It is crucial to maintain consistent tension throughout your project to ensure that the stitches are even and the design is clear. This can be achieved by practicing and paying attention to your tension as you work.

Another aspect to consider is the choice of yarn. It is recommended to use yarns with good stitch definition and contrasting colors to make the mosaic effect more pronounced. This will help the design stand out and create a visually striking finished project.

Working with Overlay Mosaic Crochet can be challenging at first, especially if you are new to the technique. However, with practice and patience, you will gradually become more comfortable and confident in creating intricate and beautiful designs.

The possibilities with Overlay Mosaic Crochet are endless. You can create anything from blankets and scarves to bags and home decor items. The technique allows you to incorporate complex patterns and motifs into your crochet projects, making them truly unique and eye-catching.

In conclusion, working with Overlay Mosaic Crochet is a rewarding and creative way to enhance your crochet skills. It offers a unique and visually stunning way to incorporate multiple colors and textures into your projects. With practice and dedication, you can create beautiful and intricate designs that will impress and inspire others. So why not give Overlay Mosaic Crochet a try and see where your creativity takes you?

Creating Illusion with Shadow Mosaic Crochet: Creating Illusion with Shadow Mosaic Crochet is a fascinating and intricate technique that allows crocheters to create stunning and visually striking designs. This technique involves using different colors of yarn to create a pattern that gives the illusion of depth and dimension, similar to a mosaic or a shadow.

The process of creating a shadow mosaic crochet piece begins with selecting a design or pattern that lends itself well to this technique. This can be anything from geometric shapes to intricate images or even portraits. Once the design is chosen, the crocheter will need to gather the necessary materials, including different colors of yarn, a crochet hook, and a pattern chart or graph.

The first step in creating a shadow mosaic crochet piece is to understand the pattern chart or graph. This chart will typically consist of a grid, with each square representing a stitch and each color representing a different yarn color. The crocheter will need to follow the chart carefully, working row by row, to create the desired design.

To create the illusion of depth and dimension, the crocheter will use a combination of single crochet stitches and slip stitches. By strategically placing these stitches in different colors, the crocheter can create the appearance of shadows and highlights within the design. This technique requires careful attention to detail and precision, as even a small mistake can disrupt the illusion.

As the crocheter progresses through the pattern, they will start to see the design come to life. The combination of colors and stitches will create a visually stunning piece that appears three-dimensional, despite being made with just yarn and a crochet hook. This technique is often used to create wall hangings, blankets, or even clothing items that are sure to impress.

While shadow mosaic crochet can be a challenging technique to master, the end result is well worth the effort. The intricate designs and stunning illusions created with this technique are sure to captivate and amaze anyone who sees them. Whether you are an experienced crocheter looking to expand your skills or a beginner eager to try something new, shadow mosaic crochet is a technique that offers endless possibilities for creativity and artistic expression.

Introduction

I learnt to crochet out of necessity when my children were tiny. With their inquisitive little fingers into absolutely everything, my beloved sewing equipment suddenly transformed itself into a danger zone: pins, scissors, sewing machine, horror! It all had to be locked safely in the cupboard and, out of desperation to stop my brain turning to mush, I reached for a crochet hook. In the early days of learning my fabulously portable hook and yarn went everywhere with me: play groups, swimming lessons, children's parties. And from the very outset I was fascinated by this craft's natural affinity with geometry. Stripes, squares, hexagons; so pleasing to the eye, so easy to achieve, so much simpler than negotiating with a three-year-old to get their shoes on. My crochet obsession was born.

It wasn't until a few years later that I saw a mosaic crochet blanket design and everything changed for me in that moment. To produce such a bold, modern, geometric design with just two colours of yarn and a hook… what was this? Surely it would be incredibly complicated, with incomprehensible stitches and a million ends to sew in. As it turned out it was actually incredibly straightforward once I'd worked out the basic techniques. And minimal ends to sew in (joy!) because this version of mosaic crochet works on a two-row method. Two rows with one colour, change to the next colour for two rows, carry the unused yarn up the side of the work. With a few basic techniques to follow, and with some squared paper to sketch my chart ideas onto, I fell down the mosaic crochet rabbit hole, and I remain there happily to this very day.

The chance to spend a whole year immersed in mosaic crochet, burning the midnight oil with my hook in hand to create the projects for a book, has been a dream come true! In This Book I aim to share my skills and passion with you, so that you too can create beautiful throws and stylish homewares whatever your crochet level. It's also a book about making these designs your own, exploring the possibilities of colour and being inspired to start your own design adventures along the way. The Understanding Mosaic Crochet section talks you through all the necessary information you'll need, including a step-by-step guide to making a simple swatch (I wholeheartedly recommend you make this swatch if you're new to mosaic crochet or need to brush up on your technique). One crochet hook and two balls of yarn are all you need to get started.

Once you're happy with the techniques and terminology (and don't forget, I use UK terms throughout), there are 24 wonderful projects to dive into. Whilst I love all the designs there are a couple of projects that have taken on special significance for me: the Tea Lover's Tea Cosy is a firm favourite, because sitting with loved ones over a cup of tea became such a rare and precious treat in the turbulent year of 2020. Similarly, the wonderfully exuberant Yes Throw is very special – it's a symbol of positivity and hope, and it will always remind me to keep making and to keep finding the joy. Regardless of whether you recreate my patterns exactly, or use them as a starting point to go down your own mosaic crochet rabbit hole, I hope you find as much enjoyment in this beautiful craft as I do, and I wish you many hours of mosaic crochet joy ahead.

Understanding mosaic crochet

I'll let you into a secret... mosaic crochet is far easier than it looks! If you can work a chain, a double crochet and a treble crochet, then you can mosaic crochet. I know many enthusiastic beginners who have got to grips with this technique in no time, despite their trepidation to begin with. So don't worry if it's all new to you; I'm going to talk you through the basic principles, then you'll find instructions for making a small step-by-step swatch if you want to practise before starting one of the main patterns. All patterns are given with full, written row-by-row instructions, and also in chart form, so you can work in your preferred way throughout the book.

This style of mosaic crochet works really well with two contrasting colours to show off the beautiful geometric designs, and it uses the simple two-row technique – this means you use one colour for two rows, then change to the other colour for the next two rows, then back to the first colour for the next two rows, and so on. The yarn not being used just hangs at the side of the work, ready to be picked up again after two rows (don't run it along the top of the work, this is not tapestry crochet). There are minimal ends to sew in because you carry the yarns up the side of the work instead of fastening them off.

GETTING STARTED

Before making a swatch, have a quick look through the Abbreviations and Repeat Formats to familiarize yourself with the main UK terms used. There are two special abbreviations that are essential for this style of mosaic crochet:

cc, change colour: to change colour, work the last double crochet (dc) of the row in the old colour up to the last two loops on the hook, then yarn round hook with the new colour and draw the new colour through the loops on the hook to finish the stitch.

mtr, mosaic treble crochet: work a treble (tr) as normal but work it in the skipped stitch of the same colour three rows below, working the stitch **in front** of the intervening two rows of chain in the other colour. The chains will be visible and loose on the back of the work. All mosaic treble are worked on the right side of the work.

Look out for the symbol at the start of every pattern, which shows you how easy or tricky the project will be.

Easy

An easy project, suitable for a crocheter with basic skills

Intermediate

An intermediate project, this may have a more complex pattern which requires more concentration

Advanced

An advanced project, involving a much more elaborate pattern. In addition, some other skills such as sewing may be required

OTHER USEFUL MOSAIC CROCHET INFORMATION

The first row of a colour 'creates' the pattern, the second row 'reinforces' it. Where a double crochet or a mosaic treble is made in the first row, a double crochet is always made in this stitch in the second row (make sure to work into all mosaic treble stitches from the first row as they can easily be missed). Where a chain-space is made in the first row, the same chain-space is made in the second row. In essence, the second row of the colour copies the first row, but uses double crochet to replace any mosaic trebles.

When making your chain-spaces, you will always make one more chain than the number of stitches being skipped: for example, to skip 1 stitch, chain 2; to skip 2 stitches, chain 3; to skip 3 stitches, chain 4 and so on. This 'extra chain' simply exists to stop the work from pulling in and becoming too tight.

Always work into the full stitch as you normally would; some mosaic crochet techniques ask you to work in back loops or front loops only, but not this version.

To adjust the length of your starting chain, use the Pattern Multiples at the start of the pattern: make your chain, then follow the pattern from Row 1. You will always have one fewer double crochet at the end of Row 1 than chains in your starting chain. For example, a starting chain of 50 means you will have 49 double crochet.

LET'S NOT GET TENSE ABOUT TENSION

Tension… it can be a real stress when working with yarn – are you using the right hook size? What about the thickness of the yarn? Are you a tight or a loose crocheter (or somewhere in between)? My general feeling for the purposes of enjoying this book is to not worry too much about it. We can be a bit flexible with dimensions of throws and tote bags, we're not making garments which have to fit exactly. So, with that in mind, refer to the Tension guide and the Measurements at the start of each pattern, but don't worry if your tension is not exactly the same as mine.

TOP TIPS FOR TENSION

- *Make a small swatch first to give you an idea of measurements.*
- *Use the Pattern Multiples at the start of the pattern to work out your starting chain, then follow the pattern from Row 1.*
- *Go up or down a hook size. Throws need a good drape, cushions and bags need a tighter fabric, so experiment with different hooks on a swatch to get it right for you and your yarn.*
- *Trust your instincts: yes, it's annoying to unravel a few starting rows of a throw, but better to get it right than to plough on if you're not happy with the drape or look of your work.*
- *Think about borders: I have added a very simple border to some of the throws in the book, but you could consider a wider, more elaborate border to add extra width and length. The same goes for cushions: if your cushion covers are coming up small, simply add a few more rounds of double crochet border in your contrast colour to adjust the sizing.*

MAKING A SWATCH

Use any suitable hook.

Using first colour, ch22. (A)

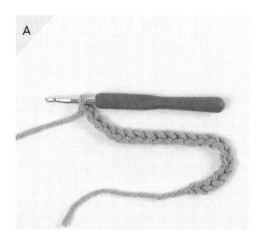

Row 1 (RS): 1dc in the second ch from the hook and in each ch to the end. (21 sts) (B)

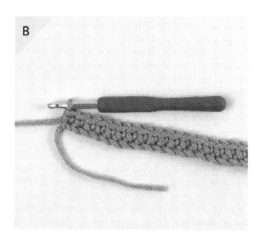

Turn work.

Row 2 (WS): Ch1 (every row from now on starts with ch1, but it never counts as a st), 1dc in each st to the last st, work the last st up to the last 2 lps on the hook (C), cc to second colour. (21 sts) (D)

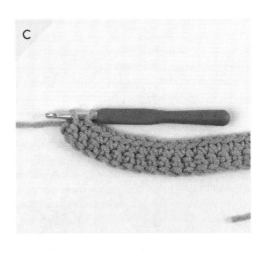

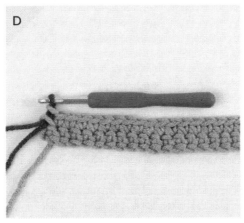

Turn work.

Leave first colour hanging at the side of the work for the next 2 rows and continue with second colour.

Row 3 (RS): Ch1, 1dc, *ch2, skip 1 st, 5dc; rep from * to the last 2 sts, ch2, skip 1 st, 1dc in the last st. (E)

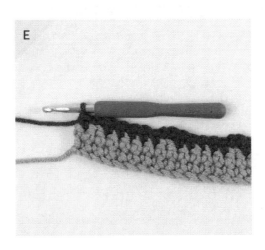

Turn work.

Row 4 (WS): Ch1, 1dc, *ch2, skip 2ch-sp, 5dc; rep from * to the last 2ch-sp and dc, ch2, skip 2ch-sp, 1dc in the last st, cc to first colour (which is hanging at the side of the work) in the last dc as before. (F)

Turn work.

Leave second colour hanging at the side of the work for the next 2 rows and continue with first colour.

Row 5 (RS): Ch1, 1dc, *1mtr in the skipped st in first colour (below the 2 rows of ch in second colour), 5dc; rep from * to the last 2ch-sp and dc, 1mtr, 1dc in the last st. (G)

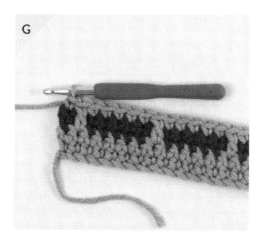

Turn work.

Row 6 (WS): Ch1, 1dc in each st to the end of the row, cc to second colour in the last st as before. (H)

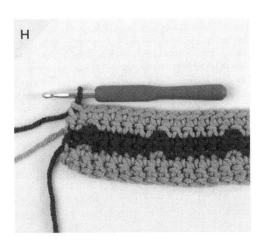

Turn work.

Leave first colour hanging at the side of the work for the next 2 rows and continue with second colour.

Rows 7–10: As Rows 3–6. Fasten off yarns, weave in ends. (I)

This swatch is the most basic form of mosaic crochet that you'll find in this book – see the skill levels on each pattern if you want to start with a simple project. Some patterns are more complex but they all work to exactly the same basic principles of working double crochet, mosaic treble and chains, and, in general, changing colour every two rows.

TOP TIP

Choose two contrasting yarn colours so you can clearly see your colour changes and stitch definition.

HOW TO FOLLOW A MOSAIC CROCHET CHART

If you find it easier to work from a chart, here are the basic principles of mosaic crochet chart-reading.

Each square represents a stitch.

Read all odd-numbered (RS) rows from right to left, and all even-numbered (WS) rows from left to right.

This chart corresponds exactly with the written swatch pattern (see Making a Swatch).

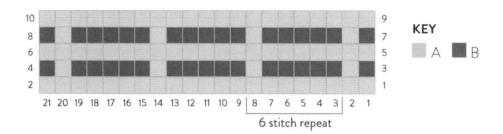

Make your starting chain, with one more chain than the number of double crochet needed in Row 1 of the chart.

Read the chart from the bottom up. Most charts are symmetrical and can be read from right to left and/or left to right. However, if the pattern is NOT symmetrical, then read the chart from right to left for the first row of a colour, and then left to right for the second row of the same colour.

Each chart row represents **TWO** rows of crochet in the same colour. The first row of a colour 'makes' the pattern, the second row of the same colour 'reinforces' it. You will see that each chart row is numbered to indicate the two rows of crochet, for example 1 on the right and 2 on the left, 3 and 4, 5 and 6 and so on.

The colour shown in the first and last squares of the chart row shows you which colour to use for these two rows. These first and last stitches will always be a double crochet. Always chain 1 at the start of each row as your turning chain, this never counts as a stitch.

Each square in a chart row represents a stitch: either a double crochet, mosaic treble, or chain-space in the first row of the colour. In the second row of that colour, always work a double crochet into a double crochet or mosaic treble from the first row, or make the same number of chain-spaces as in the first row.

When a square appears in the chart row that is a different colour from the colour in use, make a chain-space to skip the stitch(es) below. To skip one stitch, chain 2; to skip two sts, chain 3; to skip three stitches, chain 4 and so on. This 'extra chain' simply exists to stop the work from pulling in and becoming too tight. This chain-space, made in both rows of the same colour, will be filled in later with mosaic treble worked **in front** of the two rows of chain, into the skipped stitch(es) below.

SAFETY FIRST

Mosaic crochet patterns produce lengths of chain on the wrong side of the work. Although this creates a nice 'raised effect' on the right side, it makes items such as throws and scarves unsuitable to give to babies, small children and pets because there could be a choke/entanglement risk. There's an easy fix to this so please read the following instructions to show you how to eliminate these loose chains.

To hide the chain so it is not a choke/entanglement risk

Work your mtr as normal into the skipped stitch of the same colour 3 rows below, but work it **around** the intervening 2 rows of chain, so that the chain is incorporated into the mtr and therefore does not appear loose on the back. The only downside to this method is that you can see a little more of the background colour showing between the stitches. (J, K)

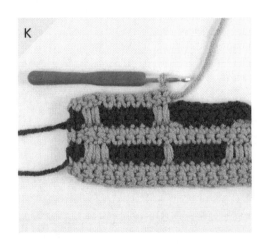

Right side   *Wrong side*

To leave the chain lying loose across the back of the work

Work your mtr as normal into the skipped stitch of the same colour 3 rows below, but work the stitch **in front of** the intervening 2 rows of chain in contrast colour, so that the mtr sits on top of the chain, and the chain is clearly visible and loose on the back. (L, M)

Right side

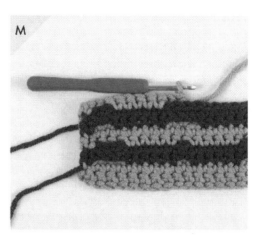

Wrong side

Materials and tools

YARN

I am extremely grateful to Scheepjes who very kindly offered me yarn support for this book. I chose to use Scheepjes yarns exclusively because, quite simply, I adore them: the quality, range and colours are second to none. Many of the throw designs in this book are made with their Colour Crafter DK range because it is excellent quality, good value, washable and 100% acrylic, which makes it perfect for large projects.

You can use any DK yarn you prefer instead, but bear in mind you might need a different quantity to the amount stated at the start of each pattern (this goes for any project with a yarn substitution, of course). It's also important to carefully consider your colour choices if you are substituting yarn and want to reproduce the same effect as mine, because even a small difference in colour tone will alter the end result. I recommend making a small swatch with the substitute yarn before you start to check that your colour choices work and that the yarn works for the project you have in mind. For a rug you'll need a hard-wearing, durable yarn; for a baby blanket something soft, easy to wash and non-allergenic would be suitable. Cushions and bags work best in tough cottons and jute mixes.

As this book is all about the flexibility of mosaic crochet, the Pattern Multiples are given at the start of every project to help you calculate your starting chain if you want to scale the project up or down to suit a particular yarn. For example, if you want to make a beautifully cosy throw in a chunky yarn but the pattern uses DK, just adjust your starting chain to the size to suit you, following the Pattern Multiples given in the pattern. There are endless options and possibilities, so you don't have to follow my exact yarn choice all the time.

HOOK

Be prepared to adjust your crochet hook size if you want your tension to match mine, as yarn thicknesses vary even under the same name; a DK from one manufacturer might not be exactly the same thickness as that from another. In addition, everyone crochets to a slightly different tension, so this needs to be taken into consideration. Look for the Tension guide at the start of the patterns for full information and adjust your hook size until you can match the tension given.

It takes many hours to make a throw, so it is important that your hook feels comfortable in your hand. There's a bewildering range of hooks out there, so it's worth trying out different makes and styles to find something that suits you. Some people like an ergonomic handle, others prefer bamboo or even hand-carved hooks. I tend to use simple, straight metal hooks as I find the yarn runs very smoothly on them. This means I can crochet quickly, which is very important when making a large throw! Whatever hook you work with, it's also essential to have regular breaks from crocheting, too, in order to give your hands a rest. Some simple finger stretches and even a soothing massage with some hand balm can soon rejuvenate your hard-working hands.

HOOK CONVERSION TABLE

METRIC SIZE	US SIZE	UK/CANADIAN SIZE
2.75mm	C/2	-
3mm	-	11
3.25mm	D/3	10
3.5mm	E/4	9
4mm	G/6	8
4.5mm	7	7
5mm	H/8	6
5.5mm	I/9	5
6mm	J/10	4
6.5mm	K10½	3
7mm	-	2
8mm	L/11	0

OTHER ITEMS

You'll need a few other supplies for some of these projects – such as pompom makers, a tape measure, lining fabric, a needle and thread, buttons and so on – but you will be able to source everything from your local haberdashery or yarn shop, or online, with no problem. You can easily make all these projects with some simple hand sewing: a sewing machine is definitely not essential! Look for the information at the start of each pattern to see what supplies you will need – everything is listed there. And remember that these patterns are the starting point for your own interpretation: if you want to make your Rebel Rainbow Tote bag without lining, simply don't line it! Maybe you prefer your cushions to have a crochet cover on both sides, rather than just on one like mine: well, adapt as you please!

Abbreviations and repeat formats

The patterns in this book use the basic crochet abbreviations listed below. These are UK crochet terms, with the corresponding US terms in the table at the end.

approx, approximately

beg, beginning

cc, change colour as follows: work last dc of row in old colour up to last 2 loops on hook, yrh with new colour and draw new colour through loops on hook

ch(s), chain(s)

ch-sp(s), chain space(s)

cont, continue(d)

dc, double crochet

dc2tog, double crochet 2 sts together (to decrease 1 st) as follows: [insert hook into next st or sp as indicated, yrh and pull a loop through] twice, yrh and pull through all 3 loops on the hook

htr, half treble crochet

lp(s), loop(s)

mtr, mosaic treble crochet as follows: tr in skipped st of same colour 3 rows below, working in front of intervening 2 rows of ch in other colour

patt, pattern

rep, repeat

RS, right side

skip, miss

slst, slip stitch

sp(s), space(s)

st(s), stitch(es)

tog, together

tr, treble crochet

WS, wrong side

yrh, yarn round hook

All the patterns in this book use repeated sections of instructions to produce the geometric patterns. Repeated sequences are indicated as follows:

*......; rep from * to, work instructions from * to ; and then repeat that section up to the point specified

*.......; rep from * once more/twice more/3 times more, work the instructions from * to ; and then repeat that section the number of times specified

[........] once/twice/3 times, work the instructions between the square brackets the total number of times specified

UK/US STITCH NAMES

UK TERM	US TERM
dc	sc
dc2tog	sc2tog
htr	hdc
tr	dc
yrh	yo

Colour considerations

Planning colours for a new project is so exciting, isn't it? That initial thrill of delving into the yarn stash or walking into a yarn shop, wondering what fabulous combinations you'll find, has to be one of the best parts of making something new. I've been working with colour (and with colour obsessives) for years, and whilst I cannot claim to be any kind of colour expert, I certainly know that many of us find putting colours together a calming and uplifting experience in a world filled with constant noise, news and stress.

My approach to working with colour is uncomplicated. I'm very much a 'less is more' designer when it comes to my colourways. I like to think of it as a modern, uncluttered look, but with a touch of quirkiness and fun added to the grown-up cool. Most of my designs use two colours, some three. A few designs use a broader palette, but this is the exception rather than the rule. Mosaic crochet is all about the stunning simplicity of geometric shapes and I want to celebrate this above all else. For me, too much colour can distract from the design and break up those gorgeous lines and angles. In some ways, the colour has to work with and show off the pattern, not the other way around. The interplay between colour and shape does take some thought and practise, so it's worth planning a bit before you pick up your hook. And once you've made your choices, I strongly recommend you make a small swatch of the design to check you're happy with how the colours actually work together before embarking on your project.

SELECTING COLOURS
When choosing colours for my own designs, I work from a very simple set of 'rules'. For example, a pale background with a main statement colour seems to work every time: Into The Trees throw uses a misty blue against a rich burnt-coppery orange and the result is breathtaking. I also adore working with neon – don't be frightened of neon colours: they can easily be calmed and tempered with other tones. Sun Spot throw does just this; its neon pink circles are vibrant but not overwhelming against the deep and serious red. Possibly my favourite colourway ever is to use a monochrome palette with a bright, popping border (pompoms and tassels welcome!), such as in the Diamonds throw and Floating Points throw. You can add a real sense fun with that dash of colour! I do occasionally broaden my palette to four or five colours within a design, but I like

them to clash somewhat. The YES throw illustrates this well with its contrasting, tonally clashing hues of pinks and yellows. But, of course, these are my colours, not yours, and you may decide they are not for you. If you're planning on going your own way and setting off on new colour adventures, but you're unsure where to start, here are my top tips:

Think about where your finished item might end up – is there a certain accent colour in this space that you love and would like as your main colour? For example, a favourite vase or a particular colour in the print on a chair might be the perfect starting point. Maybe there's an artist or a work of art that inspires you (I have photos of local graffiti which have ended up inspiring crochet!)

Or, if your item is going to be a gift for someone, consider their colours. Maybe there's a particular colour they usually wear or carry. People's scarves and other accessories often give a clue to their colour preferences as these are the personal touches we add to our outfits to express our personalities to others.

Another option is to literally stop what you're doing and open your eyes and mind to the colours around you. You'll be surprised at how many beautiful combinations you see if you look. From hanging out your socks on the washing line to spotting a beautiful bright flower growing in the cracks of the pavement, colour is all around us. Take photos of everything you like as a record, get paint charts from your local DIY shop, go online and build mood boards of beautiful interiors, fabrics, tiles, gardens – anything you see and love. You'll then have a record of beautiful combinations to turn to, to mix and match as you please, whenever the mood takes you to reach for the yarn.

COLOUR THEORY

If you want to get a bit more technical, colour theory is a fantastic, vast subject to dive into and there are many excellent books on the subject to get you started. In addition, a colour wheel can be a very inspiring tool to have at your fingertips. Complementary colours (opposite each other on the colour wheel) are really good together, such as coral and teal, or gold and plum. The same goes for a triadic scheme (three points at equal distance around the wheel) such as the primary colours red, blue and yellow.

If you need further inspiration, you'll see I've made a small swatch of each of the 12 main patterns in a new colourway to hopefully spark some fresh ideas. From an entirely monochrome palette to making your own ombré, each swatch looks at a particular colour concept. And remember, if you make a swatch to start and don't like the result, be honest and be prepared to go back to the yarn stash and start again; this is truly the best advice I can offer. Oh, that and of course have a huge amount of fun on your colourful crochet adventures!

Projects

Each of the 12 main throw designs in this section has its own spin-off project, as a way of demonstrating just how easy and flexible mosaic crochet can be. From bags and rugs to footstools and table runners, I hope you'll find the inspiration here to make your own beautiful items that will bring a cool modern vibe to your home. You'll see each project has a skill level at the start to help you choose your next project (one yarn ball for a project that's great for enthusiastic beginners, up to three yarn balls for a project that requires more concentration and maybe some sewing skills, too). Each pattern has full written instructions and also a chart, so you can choose whichever pattern-reading method suits you best. Wherever you start in this book and whichever projects you choose to make, I hope you enjoy my colourful, quirky world of mosaic crochet.

Block Party Throw

SKILL LEVEL:

Interlocking inky blue rectangles on the most beautiful washed-out blue background… there's something rather soothing and hypnotic about this design. I made so many swatches for this one with different colours, funky neons, gorgeous borders and so on, but I kept coming back to this cool, slightly grown-up colourway. Not like me at all. Sometimes the design is in charge of the designer, not the other way around it would seem…

YOU WILL NEED

YARN

Scheepjes Colour Crafter (100% acrylic), DK/light worsted, 100g (300m/328yds), in the following shades:

Goes (1820); 4 balls (A)

Tynaarlo (1011); 4 balls (B)

HOOK

5.5mm crochet hook

PATTERN MULTIPLES

Pattern works to a multiple of 10 stitches + 4 stitches for the starting chain.

TENSION (GAUGE)

15 sts and 18 rows measure 10 x 10cm (4 x 4in) over patt using a 5.5mm hook.

FINISHED SIZE

Approx. 98cm x 128cm (38½ x 50½in)

Note

A fairly straightforward mosaic pattern worked in A and B. Once the main throw is finished, the two long sides are edged in A, then tassels in B are added to each corner.

INSTRUCTIONS

Using A, ch144.

Row 1 (RS): 1dc in second ch from hook and in each ch to end, turn. (143 sts)

Row 2 (WS): Ch1 (does not count as st throughout), 1dc in each st to end, cc to B, turn.

Row 3: Ch1, 1dc, ch2, skip 1 st, *4dc, ch2, skip 1 st; rep from * to last st, 1dc, turn.

Row 4: Ch1, 1dc, ch2, skip 2ch-sp, *4dc, ch2, skip 2ch-sp; rep from * to last st, 1dc, cc to A, turn.

Row 5: Ch1, 1dc, *1mtr, ch2, skip 1 st, 3dc, 1mtr, 3dc, ch2, skip 1 st; rep from * to last 2 sts, 1mtr, 1dc, turn.

Row 6: Ch1, 2dc, *ch2, skip 2ch-sp, 7dc, ch2, skip 2ch-sp, 1dc; rep from * to last st, 1dc, cc, turn.

Row 7: Ch1, 1dc, *ch2, skip 1 st, 1mtr, ch2, skip 1 st, 5dc, ch2, skip 1 st, 1mtr; rep from * to last 2 sts, ch2, skip 1 st, 1dc, turn.

Row 8: Ch1, 1dc, *ch2, skip 2ch-sp, 1dc, ch2, skip 2ch-sp, 5dc, ch2, skip 2ch-sp, 1dc; rep from * to last 2 sts, ch2, skip 2ch-sp, 1dc, cc, turn.

Row 9: Ch1, 1dc, *1mtr, ch2, skip 1 st, 1mtr, ch6, skip 5 sts, 1mtr, ch2, skip 1 st; rep from * to last 2 sts, 1mtr, 1dc, turn.

Row 10: Ch1, 2dc, *ch2, skip 2ch-sp, 1dc, ch6, skip 6ch-sp, 1dc, ch2, skip 2ch-sp, 1dc; rep from * to last st, 1dc, cc, turn.

Row 11: Ch1, 1dc, *ch2, skip 1 st, 1mtr, ch2, skip 1 st, 5mtr, ch2, skip 1 st, 1mtr; rep from * to last 2 sts, ch2, skip 1 st, 1dc, turn.

Row 12: Ch1, 1dc, *ch2, skip 2ch-sp, 1dc, ch2, skip 2ch-sp, 5dc, ch2, skip 2ch-sp, 1dc; rep from * to last 2 sts, ch2, skip 2ch-sp, 1dc, cc, turn.

Row 13: Ch1, 1dc, *1mtr, ch2, skip 1 st, 1mtr, ch6, skip 5 sts, 1mtr, ch2, skip 1 st; rep from * to last 2 sts, 1mtr, 1dc, turn.

Row 14: Ch1, 2dc, *ch2, skip 2ch-sp, 1dc, ch6, skip 6ch-sp, 1dc, ch2, skip 2ch-sp, 1dc; rep from * to last st, 1dc, cc, turn.

Row 15: Ch1, 1dc, *ch2, skip 1 st, 1mtr, ch2, skip 1 st, 5mtr, ch2, skip 1 st, 1mtr; rep from * to last 2 sts, ch2, skip 1 st, 1dc, turn.

Row 16: Ch1, 1dc, *ch2, skip 2ch-sp, 1dc, ch2, skip 2ch-sp, 5dc, ch2, skip 2ch-sp, 1dc; rep from * to last 2 sts, ch2, skip 2ch-sp, 1dc, cc, turn.

Row 17: Ch1, 1dc, *1mtr, ch2, skip 1 st, 1mtr, 5dc, 1mtr, ch2, skip 1 st; rep from * to last 2 sts, 1mtr, 1dc, turn.

Row 18: Ch1, 2dc, *ch2, skip 2ch-sp, 7dc, ch2, skip 2ch-sp, 1dc; rep from * to last st, 1dc, cc, turn.

Row 19: Ch1, 1dc, *ch2, skip 1 st, 1mtr, 3dc, ch2, skip 1 st, 3dc, 1mtr; rep from * to last 2 sts, ch2, skip 1 st, 1dc, turn.

Row 20: Ch1, 1dc, ch2, skip 2ch-sp, *4dc, ch2, skip 2ch-sp; rep from * to last st, 1dc, cc, turn.

Row 21: Ch1, 1dc, 1mtr, 3dc, ch2, skip 1 st, 1mtr, ch2, skip 1 st, *3dc, 1mtr, 3dc, ch2, skip 1 st, 1mtr, ch2, skip 1 st; rep from * to last 5 sts, 3dc, 1mtr, 1dc, turn.

Row 22: Ch1, 5dc, ch2, skip 2ch-sp, 1dc, ch2, skip 2ch-sp, *7dc, ch2, skip 2ch-sp, 1dc, ch2, skip 2ch-sp; rep from * to last 5 sts, 5dc, cc, turn.

Row 23: Ch1, 1dc, ch2, skip 1 st, 2dc, [ch2, skip 1 st, 1mtr] twice, *ch2, skip 1 st, 5dc, [ch2, skip 1 st, 1mtr] twice; rep from * to last 5 sts, ch2, skip 1 st, 2dc, ch2, skip 1 st, 1dc, turn.

Row 24: Ch1, 1dc, ch2, skip 2ch-sp, 2dc, [ch2, skip 2ch-sp, 1dc] twice, *ch2, skip 2ch-sp, 5dc, [ch2, skip 2ch-sp, 1dc] twice; rep from * to last 5 sts, ch2, skip

2ch-sp, 2dc, ch2, skip 2ch-sp, 1dc, cc, turn.

Row 25: Ch1, 1dc, 1mtr, ch3, skip 2 sts, [1mtr, ch2, skip 1 st] twice, *1mtr, ch6, skip 5 sts, [1mtr, ch2, skip 1 st] twice; rep from * to last 5 sts, 1mtr, ch3, skip 2 sts, 1mtr, 1dc, turn.

Row 26: Ch1, 2dc, ch3, skip 3ch-sp, [1dc, ch2, skip 2ch-sp] twice, *1dc, ch6, skip 6ch-sp, [1dc, ch2, skip 2ch-sp] twice; rep from * to last 5 sts, 1dc, ch3, skip 3ch-sp, 2dc, cc, turn.

Row 27: Ch1, 1dc, ch2, skip 1 st, 2mtr, [ch2, skip 1 st, 1mtr] twice, *ch2, skip 1 st, 5mtr, [ch2, skip 1 st, 1mtr] twice; rep from * to last 5 sts, ch2, skip 1 st, 2mtr, ch2, skip 1 st, 1dc, turn.

Row 28: Ch1, 1dc, ch2, skip 2ch-sp, 2dc, [ch2, skip 2ch-sp, 1dc] twice, *ch2, skip 2ch-sp, 5dc, [ch2, skip 2ch-sp, 1dc] twice; rep from * to last 5 sts, ch2, skip 2ch-sp, 2dc, ch2, skip 2ch-sp, 1dc, cc, turn.

Row 29: Ch1, 1dc, 1mtr, ch3, skip 2 sts, [1mtr, ch2, skip 1 st] twice, *1mtr, ch6, skip 5 sts, [1mtr, ch2, skip 1 st] twice; rep from * to last 5 sts, 1mtr, ch3, skip 2 sts, 1mtr, 1dc, turn.

Row 30: Ch1, 2dc, ch3, skip 3ch-sp, [1dc, ch2, skip 2ch-sp] twice, *1dc, ch6, skip 6ch-sp, [1dc, ch2, skip 2ch-sp] twice; rep from * to last 5 sts, 1dc, ch3, skip 3ch-sp, 2dc, cc, turn.

Row 31: Ch1, 1dc, ch2, skip 1 st, 2mtr, [ch2, skip 1 st, 1mtr] twice, *ch2, skip 1 st, 5mtr, [ch2, skip 1 st, 1mtr] twice; rep from * to last 5 sts, ch2, skip 1 st, 2mtr, ch2, skip 1 st, 1dc, turn.

Row 32: Ch1, 1dc, ch2, skip 2ch-sp, 2dc, [ch2, skip 2ch-sp, 1dc] twice, *ch2, skip 2ch-sp, 5dc, [ch2, skip 2ch-sp, 1dc] twice; rep from * to last 5 sts, ch2, skip 2ch-sp, 2dc, ch2, skip 2ch-sp, 1dc, cc, turn.

Row 33: Ch1, 1dc, 1mtr, 2dc, [1mtr, ch2, skip 1 st] twice, *1mtr, 5dc, [1mtr, ch2, skip 1 st] twice; rep from * to last 5 sts, 1mtr, 2dc, 1mtr, 1dc, turn.

Row 34: Ch1, 5dc, ch2, skip 2ch-sp, 1dc, ch2, skip 2ch-sp, *7dc, ch2, skip 2ch-sp, 1dc, ch2, skip 2ch-sp; rep from * to last 5 sts, 5dc, cc, turn.

Row 35: Ch1, 1dc, ch2, skip 1 st, *3dc, 1mtr, ch2, skip 1 st, 1mtr, 3dc, ch2, skip 1 st; rep from * to last st, 1dc, turn.

Row 36: Ch1, 1dc, ch2, skip 2ch-sp, *4dc, ch2, skip 2ch-sp; rep from * to last st, 1dc, cc, turn.

Rows 37 to 228: Rep Rows 5 to 36 a further 6 times.

Row 229: Ch1, 1dc, 1mtr, *4dc, 1mtr; rep from * to last st, 1dc, turn.

Row 230: Ch1, 1dc in each st to end.

Fasten off B, do not fasten off A.

EDGING

Edging is worked along two long sides only.

First long side

Row 1 (WS): Using A and with WS facing, ch1, rotate work 90 degrees and work along first long side as follows: *1dc in each of next four row ends, skip next row end; rep from * to end, finishing on any st in rep. If last st happens to be a skipped st, just make 1dc to finish row. Turn.

Row 2 (RS): Ch1, 1dc in each st to end.

Fasten off, weave in ends.

Second long side

Row 1 (WS): With WS facing, join A with a slst in first row end on other long side, ch1, 1dc in same st, 1dc in each of next three row ends, *skip next row end, 1dc in each of next four row ends; rep from * to end, finishing on any st in rep. If last st happens to be a skipped st, just make 1dc to finish row. Turn.

Row 2 (RS): Ch1, 1dc in each st to end, turn.

Fasten off and weave in ends.

TASSELS

(make 4)

Wrap B about 30 times around a piece of card approx. 12cm (4¾in) in length. Insert a 30cm (12in) length of B under all the loops at the top, and knot tightly to fasten and secure the loops together. Cut through all the loops along the bottom edge. Tie another 30cm (12in) piece of B around all the strands (except the joining yarn at the top) approx. 3cm (1⅛in) from the top. Trim all tassel ends level.

Attach one tassel to each corner of the Throw, using the joining yarn at the top to knot securely to each corner.

Weave in all ends to finish.

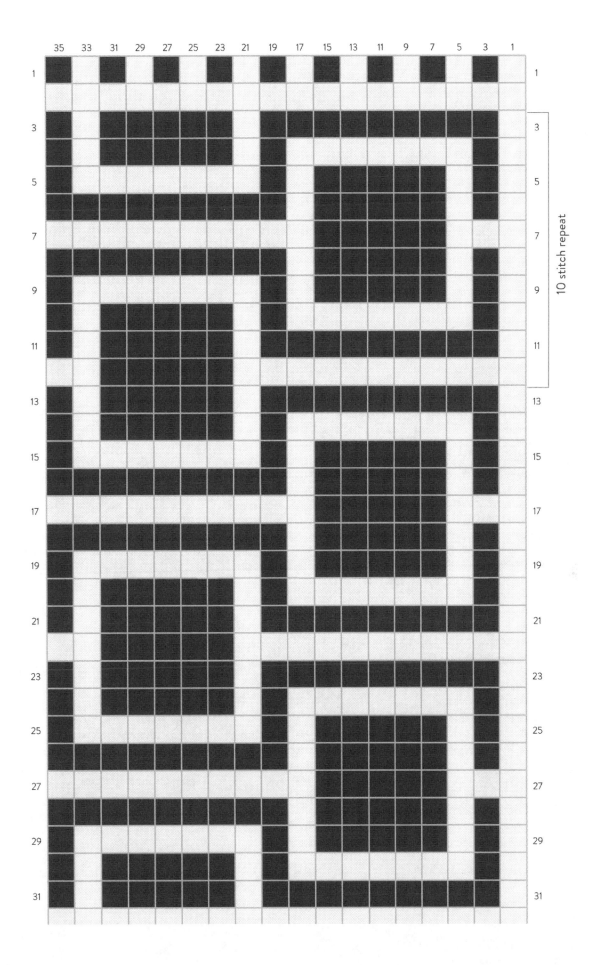

10 stitch repeat

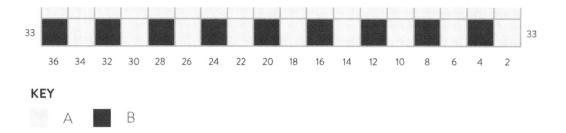

KEY

▢ A ■ B

Each square represents a stitch.

To work from this chart, rotate it 90 degrees clockwise. Read all odd-numbered (RS) rows from right to left, and all even-numbered (WS) rows from left to right.

Work rows 1 to 36 to start, and on subsequent repeats work rows 5 to 36.

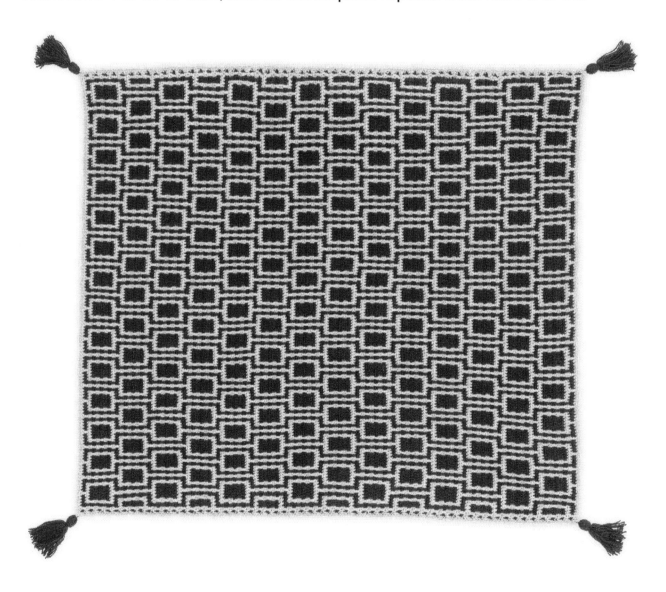

TOP TIP

You could be more rebellious than me and add an amazing bold border, and even more tassels to the ends of this throw!

Try a new colourway

LIGHTEN UP

Light colours can look bold and vibrant together if you choose one dominant colour, such as this zingy, acidic yellow. It pops so beautifully against the gorgeous soft dove grey, but it doesn't overwhelm the design.

SPIN-OFF PROJECT:

Tea Lover's Tea Cosy

Are you a tea drinker? You know, us Brits are fanatical about our cups of tea. I take teabags with me on holiday so I know I can have a PROPER cup of tea. Boiling water poured onto the teabag in the pot (which has been warmed of course), leave to brew for 3 minutes minimum, then pour into a large mug (not a cup!), add a splash of milk and no sugar please, if you'd be so kind. The pompom on top of this lovely tea cosy serves no purpose except to show off, really.

YOU WILL NEED

YARN

Scheepjes Metropolis (75% extra fine merino wool/25% nylon), 50g (200m/218yds) in the following shades:

Cota (024); 1 ball (A)

Miami (069); 1 ball (B)

Dhaka (040); 1 ball (C)

HOOK

3mm crochet hook

OTHER TOOLS AND MATERIALS

10-cup teapot: height 15cm (6in), circumference around widest part 50cm (19¾in)

85mm (3¼in) pompom maker

Button/toggle

Needle and thread

PATTERN MULTIPLES

Pattern works to a multiple of 10 stitches + 4 stitches for the starting chain.

TENSION (GAUGE)

20 sts and 26 rows measure 10 x 10cm (4 x 4in) over patt using a 3mm hook.

FINISHED SIZE

Approx. 20.5cm (8⅛in) wide x 20cm (8in) high excluding pompom

---

Notes

This tea cosy is made of two panels worked from the bottom up in A and B, with a top section worked in C on each one. A large pompom in C is attached to the top. To be able to remove the tea cosy from the pot, a loop and button are added at the back, under the bottom of the handle.

To adjust the size of the tea cosy to fit your own teapot, adjust the starting chain (see Pattern Multiples) so that the first two to three rows just fit halfway around the widest part of the tea pot (around half its 'belly' if you like). You can also go up or down a hook size, if need be, too.

INSTRUCTIONS

Panel

(make 2)

Using A, ch44.

Row 1 (RS): 1dc in second ch from hook and in each ch to end, turn. (43 sts)

Rows 2 to 36: Now follow Block Party Throw patt, starting at Row 2 (using A) and finishing at end of Row 36, using A and B as indicated.

Fasten off B.

Next row: Using A, ch1, 1dc, 1mtr, *4dc, 1mtr; rep from * to last st, 1dc, turn.

Next row: Ch1, 1dc in each st to end, cc to C, fasten off A, turn.

Top section

Row 1 (RS): Using C, ch1 (does not count as st throughout), 1dc in each st to end, turn. (43 sts)

Row 2 (WS): Ch1, 1dc, *dc2tog over next 2 sts, 1dc; rep from * to end, turn. (29 sts)

Rows 3 and 4: Ch1, 1dc in each st to end, turn.

Row 5: Ch1, dc2tog over first 2 sts, *1dc, dc2tog over next 2 sts; rep from * to end, turn. (19 sts)

Rows 6 and 7: Ch1, 1dc in each st to end, turn.

Row 8: Ch1, 1dc, *dc2tog over next 2 sts, 1dc; rep from * to end, turn. (13 sts)

Row 9: Ch1, dc2tog over first 2 sts, 1dc in each st to last 2 sts, dc2tog over last 2 sts, turn. (11 sts)

Rows 10 and 11: Ch1, 1dc in each st to end, turn.

Row 12: Ch1, 2dc, 2htr, 3tr, 2htr, 2dc, turn. (11 sts)

Row 13: Ch1, 1dc in each st to end.

Fasten off and weave in ends.

ASSEMBLY

Place both panels together with WS facing out. Thread a needle with a length of C and whip stitch across the entire edge of the top section to join the two panels together at the top. Next, thread the needle with a length of A and whip stitch from the bottom corners up the side by approx. 1cm (⅜in) to secure the two panels under the teapot spout at the front.

Fastening loop

Turn the cover to the RS, join A with a slst to one bottom edge at the back of the tea cosy, ch15 (or as many ch as needed to form your button loop), slst back into the same side, approx. 1cm (⅜in) higher up to form a loop, ch1, turn, work approx. 20dc around the chain, slst to the starting point, fasten off.

Sew the button securely on the other side at the back.

Pompom

Wrap C approx. 500 times around each side of the pompom maker to make a large pompom. Sew it securely onto the top of your tea cosy.

Weave in all ends.

TOP TIPS

- *Tea pots, like people, come in all shapes and sizes, so I've made this tea cosy easy to adapt to fit your favourite tea pot.*

- *Please take extra care when putting your tea cosy on and off the tea pot when there's hot water inside. Also, remember to keep the tea pot away from babies, small children and pets.*

Tartantastic Throw

SKILL LEVEL:

Mosaic crochet and tartan: a beautiful friendship. This chunky throw has a lot going for it and is definitely worth making if you are a lover of linear designs. It doesn't take too long to make, thanks to the beautiful thick yarn, and it just looks cool wherever you happen to fling it (in an effortlessly stylish manner of course). AND it would work in whatever palette you like – choose your five colours, grab your hook and get tartantastic! All in all, it's a total win-win design.

YOU WILL NEED

YARN

Scheepjes Chunky Monkey (100% acrylic), aran/worsted, 100g (116m/126yds), in the following shades:

Dark Grey (2018); 7 balls (A)

Cerise (1061); 1 ball (B)

Pearl Pink (1080); 3 balls (C)

Stone (2017); 3 balls (D)

Coral (1132); 1 ball (E)

HOOK

6.5mm crochet hook

PATTERN MULTIPLES

Pattern works to a multiple of 8 stitches + 4 stitches for the starting chain.

TENSION (GAUGE)

10 sts and 13 rows measure 10 x 10cm (4 x 4in) over patt using a 6.5mm hook.

FINISHED SIZE

Approx. 90 x 130 cm (35⅜ x 51in)

Note

Keep A attached to make the background colour; it will be used for two rows on, two rows off throughout. Attach and fasten off all other yarns B to E as instructed, using the Chart as required for reference.

INSTRUCTIONS

Using A, ch92.

Row 1 (RS): 1dc in second ch from hook and in each ch to end, turn. (91 sts)

Row 2 (WS): Ch1 (does not count as st throughout), 1dc in each st to end, cc to B, turn.

Row 3: Ch1, 4dc, ch2, skip 1 st, 1dc, ch2, skip 1 st, *5dc, ch2, skip 1 st, 1dc, ch2, skip 1 st; rep from * to last 4 sts, 4dc, turn.

Row 4: Ch1, 4dc, ch2, skip 2ch-sp, 1dc, ch2, skip 2ch-sp, *5dc, ch2, skip 2ch-sp, 1dc, ch2, skip 2ch-sp; rep from * to last 4 sts, 4dc, cc to A, fasten off B, turn.

Row 5: Ch1, 4dc, 1mtr, 1dc, 1mtr, *5dc, 1mtr, 1dc, 1mtr; rep from * to last 4 sts, 4dc, turn.

Row 6: Ch1, 1dc in each st to end, cc to C, turn.

Row 7: Ch1, 4dc, ch2, skip 1 st, 1dc, ch2, skip 1 st, *5dc, ch2, skip 1 st, 1dc, ch2, skip 1 st; rep from * to last 4 sts, 4dc, turn.

Row 8: Ch1, 4dc, ch2, skip 2ch-sp, 1dc, ch2, skip 2ch-sp, *5dc, ch2, skip 2ch-sp, 1dc, ch2, skip 2ch-sp; rep from * to last 4 sts, 4dc, cc to A, turn.

Row 9: Ch1, 1dc, ch4, skip 3 sts, 1mtr, ch2, skip 1 st, 1mtr, *ch6, skip 5 sts, 1mtr, ch2, skip 1 st, 1mtr; rep from * to last 4 sts, ch4, skip 3 sts, 1dc, turn.

Row 10: Ch1, 1dc, ch4, skip 4ch-sp, 1dc, ch2, skip 2ch-sp, 1dc, *ch6, skip 6ch-sp, 1dc, ch2, skip 2ch-sp, 1dc; rep from * to last 4 sts, ch4, skip 4ch-sp, 1dc, cc to C, turn.

Row 11: Ch1, 1dc, 3mtr, ch2, skip 1 st, 1mtr, ch2, skip 1 st, *5mtr, ch2, skip 1 st, 1mtr, ch2, skip 1 st; rep from * to last 4 sts, 3mtr, 1dc, turn.

Row 12: Ch1, 4dc, ch2, skip 2ch-sp, 1dc, ch2, skip 2ch-sp, *5dc, ch2, skip 2ch-sp, 1dc, ch2, skip 2ch-sp; rep from * to last 4 sts, 4dc, cc to A, fasten off C, turn.

Row 13: Ch1, 4dc, 1mtr, 1dc, 1mtr, *5dc, 1mtr, 1dc, 1mtr; rep from * to last 4 sts, 4dc, turn.

Row 14: Ch1, 1dc in each st to end, cc to D, turn.

Row 15: Ch1, 4dc, ch2, skip 1 st, 1dc, ch2, skip 1 st, *5dc, ch2, skip 1 st, 1dc, ch2, skip 1 st; rep from * to last 4 sts, 4dc, turn.

Row 16: Ch1, 4dc, ch2, skip 2ch-sp, 1dc, ch2, skip 2ch-sp, *5dc, ch2, skip 2ch-sp, 1dc, ch2, skip 2ch-sp; rep from * to last 4 sts, 4dc, cc to A, turn.

Row 17: Ch1, 1dc, ch4, skip 3 sts, 1mtr, ch2, skip 1 st, 1mtr, *ch6, skip 5 sts, 1mtr, ch2, skip 1 st, 1mtr; rep from * to last 4 sts, ch4, skip 3 sts, 1dc, turn.

Row 18: Ch1, 1dc, ch4, skip 4ch-sp, 1dc, ch2, skip 2ch-sp, 1dc, *ch6, skip 6ch-sp, 1dc, ch2, skip 2ch-sp, 1dc; rep from * to last 4 sts, ch4, skip 4ch-sp, 1dc, cc to D, turn.

Row 19: Ch1, 1dc, 3mtr, ch2, skip 1 st, 1mtr, ch2, skip 1 st, *5mtr, ch2, skip 1 st, 1mtr, ch2, skip 1 st; rep from * to last 4 sts, 3mtr, 1dc, turn.

Row 20: Ch1, 4dc, ch2, skip 2ch-sp, 1dc, ch2, skip 2ch-sp, *5dc, ch2, skip 2ch-sp, 1dc, ch2, skip 2ch-sp; rep from * to last 4 sts, 4dc, cc to A, fasten off D, turn.

Row 21: Ch1, 4dc, 1mtr, 1dc, 1mtr, *5dc, 1mtr, 1dc, 1mtr; rep from * to last 4 sts, 4dc, turn.

Row 22: Ch1, 1dc in each st to end, cc to E, turn.

Row 23: Ch1, 4dc, ch2, skip 1 st, 1dc, ch2, skip 1 st, *5dc, ch2, skip 1 st, 1dc, ch2, skip 1 st; rep from * to last 4 sts, 4dc, turn.

Row 24: Ch1, 4dc, ch2, skip 2ch-sp, 1dc, ch2, skip 2ch-sp, *5dc, ch2, skip 2ch-sp, 1dc, ch2, skip 2ch-sp; rep from * to last 4 sts, 4dc, cc to A, fasten off E, turn.

Row 25: Ch1, 4dc, 1mtr, 1dc, 1mtr, *5dc, 1mtr, 1dc, 1mtr; rep from * to last 4 sts, 4dc, turn.

Row 26: Ch1, 1dc in each st to end, cc to D, turn.

Row 27: Ch1, 4dc, ch2, skip 1 st, 1dc, ch2, skip 1 st, *5dc, ch2, skip 1 st, 1dc, ch2, skip 1 st; rep from * to last 4 sts, 4dc, turn.

Row 28: Ch1, 4dc, ch2, skip 2ch-sp, 1dc, ch2, skip 2ch-sp, *5dc, ch2, skip 2ch-sp, 1dc, ch2, skip 2ch-sp; rep from * to last 4 sts, 4dc, cc to A, turn.

Row 29: Ch1, 1dc, ch4, skip 3 sts, 1mtr, ch2, skip 1 st, 1mtr, *ch6, skip 5 sts, 1mtr, ch2, skip 1 st, 1mtr; rep from * to last 4 sts, ch4, skip 3 sts, 1dc, turn.

Row 30: Ch1, 1dc, ch4, skip 4ch-sp, 1dc, ch2, skip 2ch-sp, 1dc, *ch6, skip 6ch-sp, 1dc, ch2, skip 2ch-sp, 1dc; rep from * to last 4 sts, ch4, skip 4ch-sp, 1dc, cc to D, turn.

Row 31: Ch1, 1dc, 3mtr, ch2, skip 1 st, 1mtr, ch2, skip 1 st, *5mtr, ch2, skip 1 st, 1mtr, ch2, skip 1 st; rep from * to last 4 sts, 3mtr, 1dc, turn.

Row 32: Ch1, 4dc, ch2, skip 2ch-sp, 1dc, ch2, skip 2ch-sp, *5dc, ch2, skip 2ch-sp, 1dc, ch2, skip 2ch-sp; rep from * to last 4 sts, 4dc, cc to A, fasten off D, turn.

Row 33: Ch1, 4dc, 1mtr, 1dc, 1mtr, *5dc, 1mtr, 1dc, 1mtr; rep from * to last 4 sts, 4dc, turn.

Row 34: Ch1, 1dc in each st to end, cc to C, turn.

Row 35: Ch1, 4dc, ch2, skip 1 st, 1dc, ch2, skip 1 st, *5dc, ch2, skip 1 st, 1dc, ch2, skip 1 st; rep from * to last 4 sts, 4dc, turn.

Row 36: Ch1, 4dc, ch2, skip 2ch-sp, 1dc, ch2, skip 2ch-sp, *5dc, ch2, skip 2ch-sp, 1dc, ch2, skip 2ch-sp; rep from * to last 4 sts, 4dc, cc to A, turn.

Row 37: Ch1, 1dc, ch4, skip 3 sts, 1mtr, ch2, skip 1 st, 1mtr, *ch6, skip 5 sts, 1mtr, ch2, skip 1 st, 1mtr; rep from * to last 4 sts, ch4, skip 3 sts, 1dc, turn.

Row 38: Ch1, 1dc, ch4, skip 4ch-sp, 1dc, ch2, skip 2ch-sp, 1dc, *ch6, skip 6ch-sp, 1dc, ch2, skip 2ch-sp, 1dc; rep from * to last 4 sts, ch4, skip 4ch-sp, 1dc, cc to C, turn.

Row 39: Ch1, 1dc, 3mtr, ch2, skip 1 st, 1mtr, ch2, skip 1 st, *5mtr, ch2, skip 1 st, 1mtr, ch2, skip 1 st; rep from * to last 4 sts, 3mtr, 1dc, turn.

Row 40: Ch1, 4dc, ch2, skip 2ch-sp, 1dc, ch2, skip 2ch-sp, *5dc, ch2, skip 2ch-sp, 1dc, ch2, skip 2ch-sp; rep from * to last 4 sts, 4dc, cc to A, fasten off C, turn.

Row 41: Ch1, 4dc, 1mtr, 1dc, 1mtr, *5dc, 1mtr, 1dc, 1mtr; rep from * to last 4 sts, 4dc, turn.

Row 42: Ch1, 1dc in each st to end, cc to B, turn.

Rows 43 to 166: Rep Rows 3 to 42 a further 3 times, then rep Rows 3 to 6 once more.

Fasten off B at end of Row 166, do not fasten off A.

EDGING

Edging is worked along two long sides only.

First long side

Row 1 (WS): Using A and with WS facing, ch1, rotate work 90 degrees and work along first long side as follows: *1dc in each of next four row ends, skip next row end; rep from * to end, finishing on any st in rep. If last st happens to be a skipped st, just make 1dc to finish row. Turn.

Row 2 (RS): Ch1, 1dc in each st to end.

Fasten off and weave in ends.

Second long side

Row 1 (WS): With WS facing, join A with a slst in first row end on other long side, ch1, 1dc in same st, 1dc in each of next three row ends, *skip next row end, 1dc in each of next four row ends; rep from * to end, finishing on any st in rep. If last st happens to be a skipped st, just make 1dc to finish row. Turn.

Row 2 (RS): Ch1, 1dc in each st to end, turn.

Fasten off and weave in ends.

TASSELS

(make 4)

Wrap A about 20 times around a piece of card approx. 14cm (5½in) in length. Insert a 30cm (12in) length of A under all the loops at the top, knot tightly to fasten and secure the loops together. Cut through all the loops along the bottom edge. Tie another 30cm (12in) length of A around all the strands (except the joining yarn at the top) approx. 3cm (1⅛in) from the top. Then tie another 20cm (8in) length of A around all strands approx. 3cm (1⅛in) under that to create a 'double bobble'. Trim tassel to level off.

Attach one tassel to each corner, using the joining yarn to knot securely to the edge.

Weave in all ends to finish.

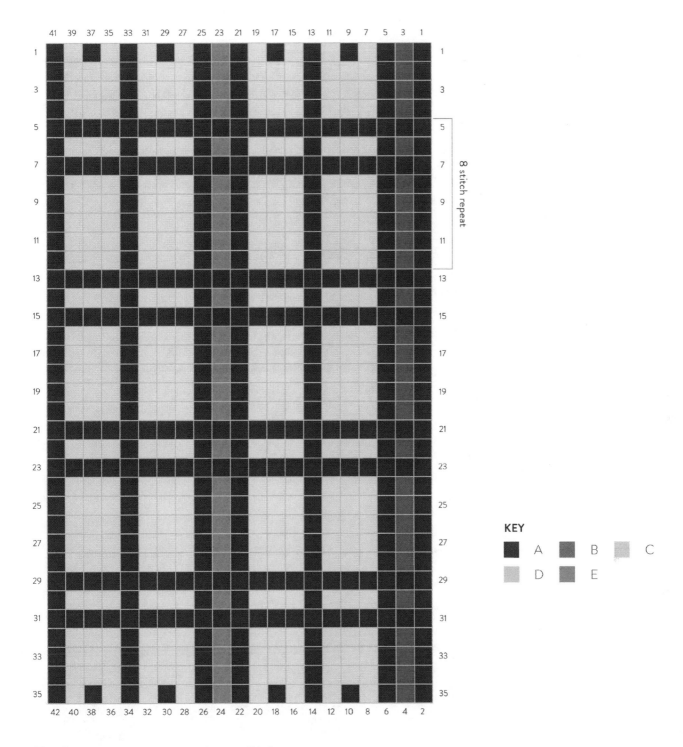

KEY

■ A   ■ B   ▨ C
▨ D   ■ E

Each square represents a stitch.

To work from this chart, rotate it by 90 degrees clockwise. Read all odd-numbered (RS) rows from right to left, and all even-numbered (WS) rows from left to right.

Work rows 1 to 42 to start, and on subsequent repeats work rows 3 to 42.

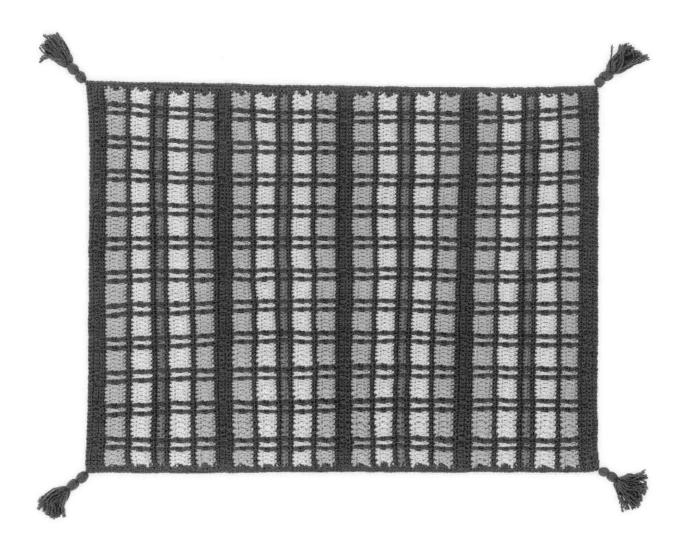

TOP TIP

This would make a fantastic over-sized winter scarf – just adjust the starting chain as required using the pattern multiples.

Try a new colourway

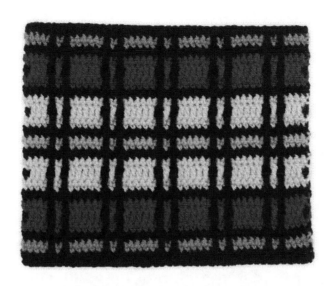

PRIMARY COLOURS

Back to primary basics here with red, yellow and blue. It's an iconic, timeless combination, which somehow manages to look modern and retro at the same time. And this linear design is, of course, doffing its cap to the work of Dutch painter Mondrian.

SPIN-OFF PROJECT:
Great Outdoors Picnic Set

Make a flask of coffee and set off with your blanket in its handy carry handle and your mugs in their stripey cosies. Whether your great outdoors is an urban bench or a field in the middle of nowhere, it's great to get out there and enjoy some fresh air.

YOU WILL NEED

YARN

Scheepjes Stone Washed XL (70% cotton/30% acrylic), aran/worsted, 50g (75m/82yds), in the following shades:

Pink Quartzite (861); 9 balls (A)

Crystal Quartz (854); 1 ball (B)

Yellow Jasper (849); 4 balls (C)

Smokey Quartz (842); 4 balls (D)

Lemon Quartz (852); 1 ball (E)

HOOKS

4.5mm crochet hook

5.5mm crochet hook

OTHER TOOLS AND MATERIALS
Carry handle

Two camping mugs, any size

Two wooden buttons or toggles

Needle and thread

PATTERN MULTIPLES

Picnic blanket: Pattern works to a multiple of 8 stitches + 4 stitches for the starting chain.

TENSION (GAUGE)

12 sts and 16 rows measure 10 x 10cm (4 x 4in) over patt using a 5.5mm hook.

FINISHED SIZE

Picnic blanket measures approx. 78cm x 105cm (31 x 41¼in) excluding tassels

---

Note

The picnic blanket is a mini version of the Tartantastic Throw, rotated 90 degrees so the length becomes the width. A row of tassels is added along each short end to finish. The mug cosies use any leftover yarn from the blanket and are very easy to customize.

INSTRUCTIONS
Picnic blanket

Using A and 5.5mm hook, ch124.

Row 1 (RS): 1dc in second ch from hook and in each ch to end, turn. (123 sts)

Rows 2 to 42: Now follow Tartantastic Throw patt, starting at Row 2 (using A) and finishing at end of Row 42, using A to E as indicated.

Rows 43 to 126: Rep Rows 3 to 42 of Tartantastic Throw patt twice more, then rep Rows 3 to 6 of Tartantastic Throw patt once more. Fasten off B at end of Row 126, do not fasten off A.

Weave in all ends before edging.

EDGING

Edge two short rows in A using same method as for Tartantastic Throw.

TASSEL FRINGE

(make 51 per short side, or as many as you like)

Cut two 12cm (4¾in) lengths of A, and fold in half. Poke the looped end through the first st at the end of a short side of the blanket. Thread the cut ends of yarn through the loop, then pull them all the way through to finish. Rep in every other st along each short end. Trim to neaten up.

Roll up the blanket and place into the carry handle.

MUG COSIES

(make 2)

Using any colour and 4.5mm hook, ch36 (or as needed to make chain 3cm/1⅛in shorter than mug circumference).

Row 1 (RS): 1dc in second ch from hook and in each ch to end, turn. (35 sts)

Following rows: Ch1, 1dc in each st to end, turn, changing yarn at end of any row to make stripes.

Work until mug cosy is slightly shorter than height of mug.

Fasten off and weave in ends.

EDGING AND BUTTON LOOP

With RS facing, join any colour with a slst in top right hand corner, slst along top edge to corner, ch1, slst in each row-end to halfway down side, ch10 to make button loop, slst in next row-end and along to corner, ch1, slst along bottom edge, ch1, slst up other side, ch1, slst to beg slst.

Fasten off and weave in ends.

Sew button in centre of other short edge to match loop.

TOP TIP

Make your mug cosies in different stripe combinations so there are no arguments whose mug is whose!

Bumblebee Throw

What is it about bumblebees that makes them so brilliant to watch? During the summer I was working on this throw I kept being distracted by these placid, ambling bees and wondering how on earth they could possibly fly – they're so furry and heavy and slow. It's like getting on a plane and worrying about how heavy it is and how it's actually going to leave the ground. Physics was never my strongest subject, obviously. This throw is my way of saying thank you to the beautiful bumblebees for their amazing gravity-defying tricks. They reminded me there's always joy and wonderment in the world, even if you've got to look a bit harder for it.

YOU WILL NEED

YARN

Scheepjes Chunky Monkey (100% acrylic), aran/worsted, 100g (116m/126yds), in the following shades:

Bumblebee (1712); 6 balls (A)

Stone (2017); 5 balls (B)

Dark Grey (2018); 2 balls (C)

HOOK

7mm crochet hook

PATTERN MULTIPLES

Pattern works to a multiple of 20 stitches + 6 stitches for the starting chain.

TENSION (GAUGE)

10 sts and 12 rows measure 10 x 10cm (4 x 4in) over patt using a 7mm hook.

FINISHED SIZE

Approx. 92 x 132cm (36 x 52in)

Note

Once the main throw is worked in A and B, four rounds of edging in C are added, then a simple tassel in C is attached to each corner to finish.

INSTRUCTIONS

Using A, ch86.

Row 1 (RS): 1dc in second ch from hook and in each ch to end, turn. (85 sts)

Row 2 (WS): Ch1 (does not count as st throughout), 1dc in each st to end, cc to B, turn.

Row 3: Ch1, 1dc, [ch2, skip 1 st, 1dc] 5 times, ch4, skip 3 sts, *1dc, [ch2, skip 1 st, 1dc] 8 times, ch4, skip 3 sts; rep from * to last 11 sts, 1dc, [ch2, skip 1 st, 1dc] 5 times, turn.

Row 4: Ch1, 1dc, [ch2, skip 2ch-sp, 1dc] 5 times, ch4, skip 4ch-sp, *1dc, [ch2, skip 2ch-sp, 1dc] 8 times, ch4, skip 4ch-sp; rep from * to last 11 sts, [1dc, ch2, skip 2ch-sp] 5 times, 1dc, cc to Yarn A, turn.

Row 5: Ch1, 1dc, [1mtr, ch2, skip 1 st] 4 times, 1mtr, 1dc, 3mtr, 1dc, 1mtr, *[ch2, skip 1 st, 1mtr] 7 times, 1dc, 3mtr, 1dc, 1mtr; rep from * to last 9 sts, [ch2, skip 1 st, 1mtr] 4 times, 1dc, turn.

Row 6: Ch1, 1dc, [1dc, ch2, skip 2ch-sp] 4 times, 7dc, *ch2, skip 2ch-sp, [1dc, ch2, skip 2ch-sp] 6 times, 7dc; rep from * to last 9 sts, [ch2, skip 2ch-sp, 1dc] 4 times, 1dc, cc, turn.

Row 7: Ch1, 1dc, [ch2, skip 1 st, 1mtr] 4 times, ch8, skip 7 sts, *1mtr, [ch2, skip 1 st, 1mtr] 6 times, ch8, skip 7 sts; rep from * to last 9 sts, [1mtr, ch2, skip 1 st] 4 times, 1dc, turn.

Row 8: Ch1, 1dc, [ch2, skip 2ch-sp, 1dc] 4 times, ch8, skip 8ch-sp, *1dc, [ch2, skip 2ch-sp, 1dc] 6 times, ch8, skip 8ch-sp; rep from * to last 9 sts, [1dc, ch2, skip 2ch-sp] 4 times, 1dc, cc, turn.

Row 9: Ch1, 1dc, 1mtr, [ch2, skip 1 st, 1mtr] 3 times, 1dc, 7mtr, 1dc, 1mtr, *[ch2, skip 1 st, 1mtr] 5 times, 1dc, 7mtr, 1dc, 1mtr; rep from * to last 7 sts, [ch2, skip 1 st, 1mtr] 3 times, 1dc, turn.

Row 10: Ch1, 1dc, [1dc, ch2, skip 2ch-sp] 3 times, 11dc, *ch2, skip 2ch-sp, [1dc, ch2, skip 2ch-sp] 4 times, 11dc; rep from * to last 7 sts, [ch2, skip 2ch-sp, 1dc] 3 times, 1dc, cc, turn.

Row 11: Ch1, 1dc, [ch2, skip 1 st, 1mtr] 3 times, ch6, skip 5 sts, 1dc, ch6, skip 5 sts, *1mtr, [ch2, skip 1 st, 1mtr] 4 times, ch6, skip 5 sts, 1dc, ch6, skip 5 sts; rep from * to last 7 sts, [1mtr, ch2, skip 1 st] 3 times, 1dc, turn.

Row 12: Ch1, 1dc, [ch2, skip 2ch-sp, 1dc] 3 times, ch6, skip 6ch-sp, 1dc, ch6, skip 6ch-sp, *1dc, [ch2, skip 2ch-sp, 1dc] 4 times, ch6, skip 6ch-sp, 1dc, ch6, skip 6ch-sp; rep from * to last 7 sts, [1dc, ch2, skip 2ch-sp] 3 times, 1dc, cc, turn.

Row 13: Ch1, 1dc, 1mtr, [ch2, skip 1 st, 1mtr] twice, 1dc, 5mtr, ch2, skip 1 st, 5mtr, 1dc, 1mtr, *[ch2, skip 1 st, 1mtr] 3 times, 1dc, 5mtr, ch2, skip 1 st, 5mtr, 1dc, 1mtr; rep from * to last 5 sts, [ch2, skip 1 st, 1mtr] twice, 1dc, turn.

Row 14: Ch1, 1dc, [1dc, ch2, skip 2ch-sp] twice, 7dc, ch2, skip 2ch-sp, 7dc, *[ch2, skip 2ch-sp, 1dc] twice, [ch2, skip 2ch-sp, 7dc] twice; rep from * to last 5 sts, [ch2, skip 2ch-sp, 1dc] twice, 1dc, cc, turn.

Row 15: Ch1, 1dc, [ch2, skip 1 st, 1mtr] twice, ch6, skip 5 sts, 1dc, ch2, skip 1 st, 1mtr, ch2, skip 1 st, 1dc, ch6, skip 5 sts, *1mtr, [ch2, skip 1 st, 1mtr] twice, ch6, skip 5 sts, 1dc, ch2, skip 1 st, 1mtr, ch2, skip 1 st, 1dc, ch6, skip 5 sts; rep from * to last 5 sts, [1mtr, ch2, skip 1 st] twice, 1dc, turn.

Row 16: Ch1, *1dc, [ch2, skip 2ch-sp, 1dc] twice, ch6, skip 6ch-sp; rep from * to last 5 sts, [1dc, ch2, skip 2ch-sp] twice, 1dc, cc, turn.

Row 17: Ch1, 1dc, 1mtr, *ch2, skip 1 st, 1mtr, 1dc, 5mtr, ch2, skip 1 st, [1mtr, ch2, skip 1 st] twice, 5mtr, 1dc, 1mtr; rep from * to last 3 sts, ch2, skip 1 st, 1mtr, 1dc, turn.

Row 18: Ch1, 2dc, *ch2, skip 2ch-sp, 7dc, ch2, skip 2ch-sp, [1dc, ch2, skip 2ch-sp] twice, 7dc; rep from * to last 3 sts, ch2, skip 2ch-sp, 2dc, cc, turn.

Row 19: Ch1, 1dc, ch2, skip 1 st, *1mtr, ch6, skip 5 sts, 1dc, ch2, skip 1 st, [1mtr, ch2, skip 1 st] 3 times, 1dc, ch6, skip 5 sts; rep from * to last 3 sts, 1mtr, ch2, skip 1 st, 1dc, turn.

Row 20: Ch1, 1dc, ch2, skip 2ch-sp, *1dc, ch6, skip 6ch-sp, 1dc, [ch2, skip 2ch-sp, 1dc] 4 times, ch6, skip 6ch-sp; rep from * to last 3 sts, 1dc, ch2, skip 2ch-sp, 1dc, cc, turn.

Row 21: Ch1, 1dc, 1mtr, *1dc, 5mtr, ch2, skip 1 st, [1mtr, ch2, skip 1 st] 4 times, 5mtr; rep from * to last 3 sts, 1dc, 1mtr, 1dc, turn.

Row 22: Ch1, 8dc, ch2, skip 2ch-sp, [1dc, ch2, skip 2ch-sp] 4 times, *11dc, ch2, skip 2ch-sp, [1dc, ch2, skip 2ch-sp] 4 times; rep from * to last 8 sts, 8dc, cc, turn.

Row 23: Ch1, 1dc, ch6, skip 5 sts, 1dc, ch2, skip 1 st [1mtr, ch2, skip 1 st] 5 times, 1dc, *ch8, skip 7 sts, 1dc, ch2, skip 1 st [1mtr, ch2, skip 1 st] 5 times, 1dc; rep from * to last 6 sts, ch6, skip 5 sts, 1dc, turn.

Row 24: Ch1, 1dc, ch6, skip 6ch-sp, 1dc, [ch2, skip 2ch-sp, 1dc] 6 times, *ch8, skip 8ch-sp, 1dc, [ch2, skip 2ch-sp, 1dc] 6 times; rep from * to last 6 sts, ch6, skip 6ch-sp, 1dc, cc, turn.

Row 25: Ch1, 1dc, 5mtr, ch2, skip 1 st, [1mtr, ch2, skip 1 st] 6 times, *7mtr, ch2, skip 1 st, [1mtr, ch2, skip 1 st] 6 times; rep from * to last 6 sts, 5mtr, 1dc, turn.

Row 26: Ch1, 6dc, ch2, skip 2ch-sp, [1dc, ch2, skip 2ch-sp] 6 times, *7dc, ch2, skip 2ch-sp, [1dc, ch2, skip 2ch-sp] 6 times; rep from * to last 6 sts, 6dc, cc, turn.

Row 27: Ch1, 1dc, *ch4, skip 3 sts, 1dc, ch2, skip 1 st, [1mtr, ch2, skip 1 st] 7 times, 1dc; rep from * to last 4 sts, ch4, skip 3 sts, 1dc, turn.

Row 28: Ch1, 1dc, *ch4, skip 4ch-sp, 1dc, [ch2, skip 2ch-sp, 1dc] 8 times; rep from * to last 4 sts, ch4, skip 4ch-sp, 1dc, cc, turn.

Row 29: Ch1, 1dc, *3mtr, 1dc, 1mtr, [ch2, skip 1 st, 1mtr] 7 times, 1dc; rep from * to last 4 sts, 3mtr, 1dc, turn.

Row 30: Ch1, 6dc, ch2, skip 2ch-sp, [1dc, ch2, skip 2ch-sp] 6 times, *7dc, ch2, skip 2ch-sp, [1dc, ch2, skip 2ch-sp] 6 times; rep from * to last 6 sts, 6dc, cc, turn.

Row 31: Ch1, 1dc, ch6, skip 5 sts, 1mtr, [ch2, skip 1 st, 1mtr] 6 times, *ch8, skip 7 sts, 1mtr, [ch2, skip 1 st, 1mtr] 6 times; rep from * to last 6 sts, ch6, skip 5 sts, 1dc, turn.

Row 32: Ch1, 1dc, ch6, skip 6ch-sp, 1dc, [ch2, skip 2ch-sp, 1dc] 6 times, *ch8, skip 8ch-sp, 1dc, [ch2, skip 2ch-sp, 1dc] 6 times; rep from * to last 6 sts, ch6, skip 6ch-sp, 1dc, cc, turn.

Row 33: Ch1, 1dc, 5mtr, 1dc, 1mtr, [ch2, skip 1 st, 1mtr] 5 times, 1dc, *7mtr, 1dc, 1mtr, [ch2, skip 1 st, 1mtr] 5 times, 1dc; rep from * to last 6 sts, 5mtr, 1dc, turn.

Row 34: Ch1, 8dc, ch2, skip 2ch-sp, [1dc, ch2, skip 2ch-sp] 4 times, *11dc, ch2, skip 2ch-sp, [1dc, ch2, skip 2ch-sp] 4 times; rep from * to last 8 sts, 8dc, cc, turn.

Row 35: Ch1, 1dc, ch2, skip 1 st, 1dc, ch6, skip 5 sts, 1mtr, [ch2, skip 1 st, 1mtr] 4 times, ch6, skip 5 sts, 1dc, *ch6, skip 5 sts, 1mtr, [ch2, skip 1 st, 1mtr] 4 times, ch6, skip 5 sts, 1dc; rep from * to last 2 sts, ch2, skip 1 st, 1dc, turn.

Row 36: Ch1, 1dc, ch2, skip 2ch-sp, *1dc, ch6, skip 6ch-sp, 1dc, [ch2, skip 2ch-sp, 1dc] 4 times, ch6, skip 6ch-sp; rep from * to last 3 sts, 1dc, ch2, skip 2ch-sp, 1dc, cc, turn.

Row 37: Ch1, 1dc, 1mtr, ch2, skip 1 st, *5mtr, 1dc, 1mtr, [ch2, skip 1 st, 1mtr] 3 times, 1dc, 5mtr, ch2, skip 1 st; rep from * to last 2 sts, 1mtr, 1dc, turn.

Row 38: Ch1, 2dc, *ch2, skip 2ch-sp, 7dc, ch2, skip 2ch-sp, [1dc, ch2, skip 2ch-sp] twice, 7dc; rep from * to last 3 sts, ch2, skip 2ch-sp, 2dc, cc, turn.

Row 39: Ch1, *1dc, ch2, skip 1 st, 1mtr, ch2, skip 1 st, 1dc, ch6, skip 5 sts, 1mtr, [ch2, skip 1 st, 1mtr] twice, ch6, skip 5 sts; rep from * to last 5 sts, 1dc, ch2, skip 1 st, 1mtr, ch2, skip 1 st, 1dc, turn.

Row 40: Ch1, *1dc, [ch2, skip 2ch-sp, 1dc] twice, ch6, skip 6ch-sp; rep from * to last 5 sts, [1dc, ch2, skip 2ch-sp] twice, 1dc, cc, turn.

Row 41: Ch1, 1dc, [1mtr, ch2, skip 1 st] twice, 5mtr, 1dc, 1mtr, ch2, skip 1 st, 1mtr, 1dc, 5mtr, *ch2, skip 1 st, [1mtr, ch2, skip 1 st] twice, 5mtr, 1dc, 1mtr, ch2, skip 1 st, 1mtr, 1dc, 5mtr; rep from * to last 5 sts, [ch2, skip 1 st, 1mtr] twice, 1dc, turn.

Row 42: Ch1, 1dc, [1dc, ch2, skip 2ch-sp] twice, 7dc, ch2, skip 2ch-sp, 7dc, * [ch2, skip 2ch-sp, 1dc] twice, [ch2, skip 2ch-sp, 7dc] twice; rep from * to last 5 sts, [ch2, skip 2ch-sp, 1dc] twice, 1dc, cc, turn.

Row 43: Ch1, 1dc, [ch2, skip 1 st, 1mtr] twice, ch2, skip 1 st, 1dc, ch6, skip 5 sts, 1mtr, ch6, skip 5 sts, *1dc, [ch2, skip 1 st, 1mtr] 3 times, ch2, skip 1 st, 1dc, ch6, skip 5 sts, 1mtr, ch6, skip 5 sts; rep from * to last 7 sts, 1dc, [ch2, skip 1 st, 1mtr] twice, ch2, skip 1 st, 1dc, turn.

Row 44: Ch1, 1dc, [ch2, skip 2ch-sp, 1dc] 3 times, ch6, skip 6ch-sp, 1dc, ch6, skip 6ch-sp, *1dc, [ch2, skip 2ch-sp, 1dc] 4 times, ch6, skip 6ch-sp, 1dc, ch6, skip 6ch-sp; rep from * to last 7 sts, [1dc, ch2, skip 2ch-sp] 3 times, 1dc, cc, turn.

Row 45: Ch1, 1dc, [1mtr, ch2, skip 1 st] 3 times, 5mtr, 1dc, 5mtr, *ch2, skip 1 st, [1mtr, ch2, skip 1 st] 4 times, 5mtr, 1dc, 5mtr; rep from * to last 7 sts, [ch2, skip 1 st, 1mtr] 3 times, 1dc, turn.

Row 46: Ch1, 1dc, [1dc, ch2, skip 2ch-sp] 3 times, 11dc, *ch2, skip 2ch-sp, [1dc, ch2, skip 2ch-sp] 4 times, 11dc; rep from * to last 7 sts, [ch2, skip 2ch-sp, 1dc] 3 times, 1dc, cc, turn.

Row 47: Ch1, 1dc, [ch2, skip 1 st, 1mtr] 3 times, ch2, skip 1 st, 1dc, ch8, skip 7 sts, *1dc, [ch2, skip 1 st, 1mtr] 5 times, ch2, skip 1 st, 1dc, ch8, skip 7 sts; rep from * to last 9 sts, 1dc, [ch2, skip 1 st, 1mtr] 3 times, ch2, skip 1 st, 1dc, turn.

Row 48: Ch1, 1dc, [ch2, skip 2ch-sp, 1dc] 4 times, ch8, skip 8ch-sp, *1dc, [ch2, skip 2ch-sp, 1dc] 6 times, ch8, skip 8ch-sp; rep from * to last 9 sts, [1dc, ch2, skip 2ch-sp] 4 times, 1dc, cc, turn.

Row 49: Ch1, 1dc, [1mtr, ch2, skip 1 st] 4 times, 7mtr, *ch2, skip 1 st, [1mtr, ch2, skip 1 st] 6 times, 7mtr; rep from * to last 9 sts, [ch2, skip 1 st, 1mtr] 4 times, 1dc, turn.

Row 50: Ch1, 1dc, [1dc, ch2, skip 2ch-sp] 4 times, 7dc, *ch2, skip 2ch-sp, [1dc, ch2, skip 2ch-sp] 6 times, 7dc; rep from * to last 9 sts, [ch2, skip 2ch-sp, 1dc] 4 times, 1dc, cc, turn.

Row 51: Ch1, 1dc, [ch2, skip 1 st, 1mtr] 4 times, ch2, skip 1 st, 1dc, ch4, skip 3 sts, *1dc, [ch2, skip 1 st, 1mtr] 7 times, ch2, skip 1 st, 1dc, ch4, skip 3 sts; rep from * to last 11 sts, 1dc, [ch2, skip 1 st, 1mtr] 4 times, ch2, skip 1 st, 1dc, turn.

Row 52: Ch1, 1dc, [ch2, skip 2ch-sp, 1dc] 5 times, ch4, skip 4ch-sp, *1dc, [ch2, skip 2ch-sp, 1dc] 8 times, ch4, skip 4ch-sp; rep from * to last 11 sts, [1dc, ch2, skip 2ch-sp] 5 times, 1dc, cc, turn.

Rows 53 to 148: Rep Rows 5 to 52 twice more.

Row 149: Ch1, [1dc, 1mtr] 5 times, 1dc, 3mtr, *[1dc, 1mtr] 8 times, 1dc, 3mtr; rep from * to last 11 sts, [1dc, 1mtr] 5 times, 1dc, turn.

Row 150: Ch1, 1dc in each st to end.

Fasten off and weave in ends.

EDGING

Round 1 (RS): Join C with a slst in top right hand st on edge of throw, ch1 (does not count as st throughout), (1dc, ch2, 1dc) in same st, 1dc in each st to last st on top edge, (1dc, ch2, 1dc) in last st, rotate work 90 degrees, 1dc in each of next three row ends, *skip next row end, 1dc in each of next four row ends; rep from * to end of long side, finishing on any st in rep, rotate work, (1dc, ch2, 1dc) in first st on bottom edge, 1dc in each st to last st on bottom edge, (1dc, ch2, 1dc) in last st, rotate work, 1dc in each of next three row ends, **skip next row end, 1dc in each of next four row ends; rep from ** to end of long side, finishing on any st in rep, slst to beg dc, turn.

Round 2 (WS): Ch1, *1dc in each st to 2ch-sp, (1dc, ch2, 1dc) in ch-sp; rep from * around to end, slst to beg dc, turn.

Round 3 (RS): Ch1, *1dc in each st to 2ch-sp, (1dc, ch2, 1dc) in ch-sp; rep from * around to last side, 1dc in each st to end, slst to beg dc, turn.

Round 4 (WS): As Row 2.

Fasten off, weave in ends.

TASSELS

(make 4)

Cut sixteen 28cm lengths of C, hold them together and fold them in half, poke the looped end a short way through the 2ch-sp at the corner. Take the cut ends of yarn and thread them through the loop, then pull them gently all the way through to secure the tassel. Repeat for each corner. Trim tassels to the same length to finish.

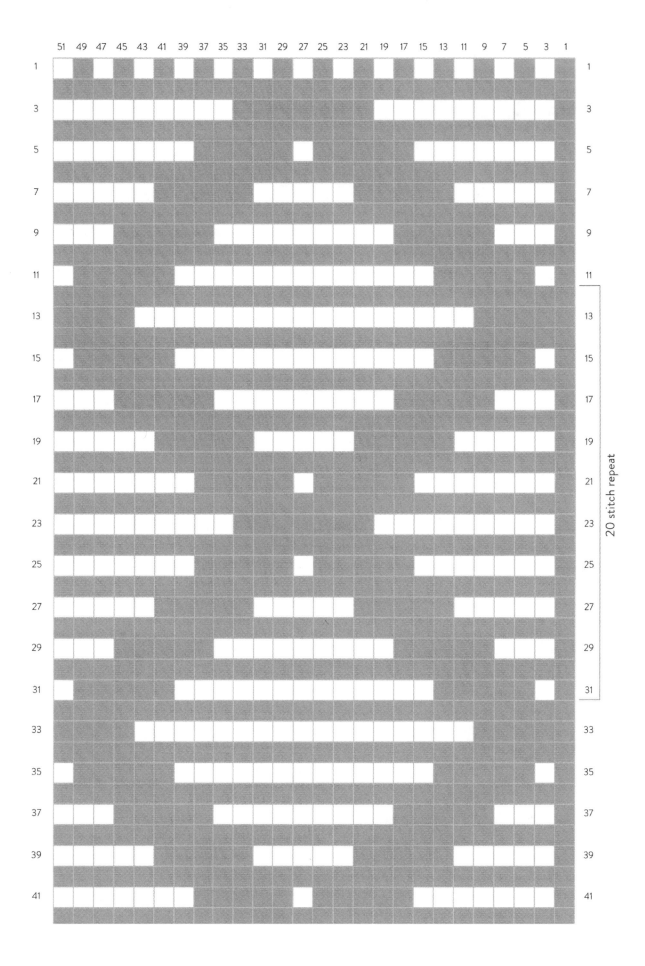

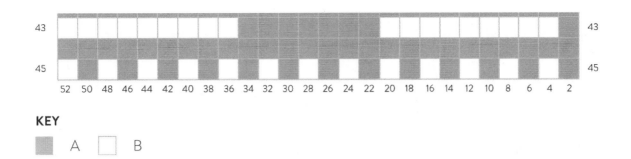

KEY

A   B

Each square represents a stitch.

To work from this chart, rotate it 90 degrees clockwise. Read all odd-numbered (RS) rows from right to left, and all even-numbered (WS) rows from left to right.

Work rows 1 to 52 to start, and on subsequent repeats work rows 5 to 52.

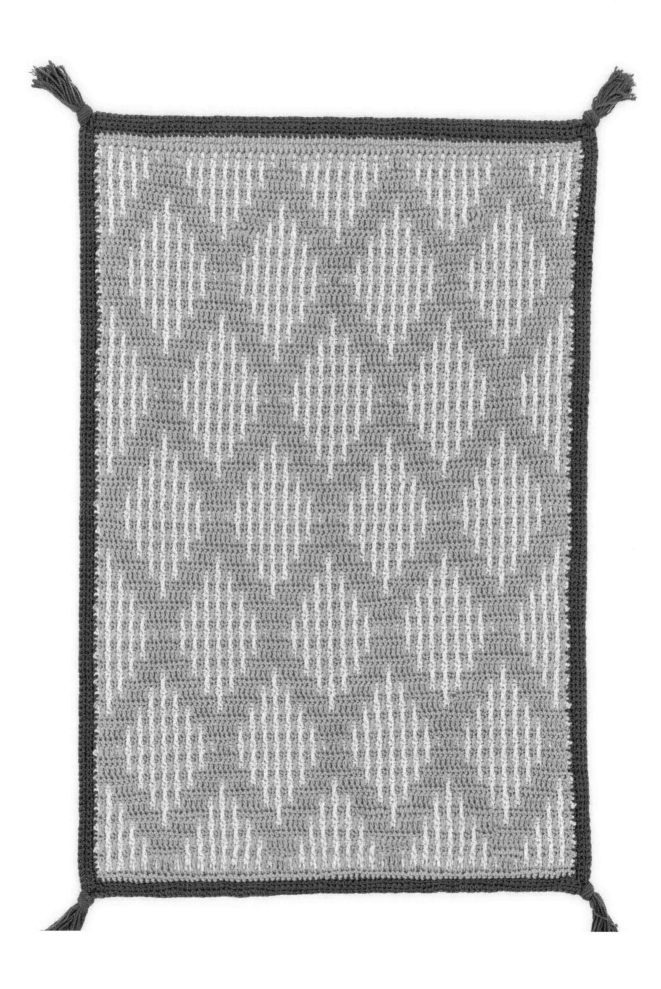

TOP TIP

A quick make with a large hook and gorgeous chunky yarn.

Try a new colourway

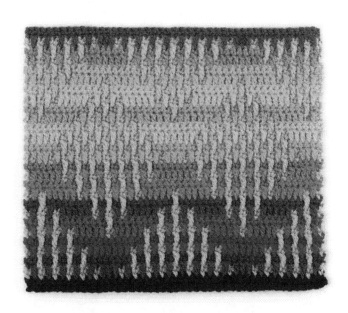

RAINBOW DAZE

Everyone loves a rainbow; hope and good fortune! Making a rainbow is a great way to stash-bust too: dig out all those colours, lay them out in an order to your liking, then simply change colour every couple of rows.

SPIN-OFF PROJECT:
Dragonfly Floor Cushion

SKILL LEVEL:

After watching the bumblebees buzzing around, which inspired the Bumblebee Throw, it seemed only fair to make something in fabulous dragonfly colours, since we are lucky to have dragonflies darting around our garden all summer. Hence the beautiful greens of this big floor cushion, with a flash of shimmering orange around the edge. Cats seem particularly keen on the floor-lounging experience and Hank Deluxe has already claimed this cushion as his own!

YOU WILL NEED

YARN

Scheepjes Metropolis (75% extra fine merino wool/25% nylon), 4-ply/sport, 50g (200m/218yds) in the following shades:

Karachi (016); 4 balls (A)

Monterrey (023); 3 balls (B)

Sevilla (076); 1 ball (C)

HOOK

4mm crochet hook

OTHER TOOLS AND MATERIALS

75cm (29½in) square floor cushion pad

77cm (30¼in) square of sturdy backing fabric

Sewing needle, thread and pins

PATTERN MULTIPLES

Pattern works to a multiple of 20 stitches + 6 stitches for the starting chain.

TENSION (GAUGE)

17 sts and 23 rows measure 10 x 10cm (4 x 4in) over patt on a 4mm hook.

FINISHED SIZE

Front measures approx. 74 x 74cm (29 x 29in)

Cushion measures 75 x 75cm (29½ x 29½in) once assembled

Notes

This floor cushion is made of a crocheted front (worked in A and B, with an edging in C) with a fabric backing; they are sewn together and a cushion pad is inserted. The crocheted cover should measure very slightly smaller than the finished cushion dimensions because you want it to stretch a little to keep its shape. If you find your cover is much smaller at the end of Row 174, make a few more rounds of double crochet edging in C than indicated to bring it to the correct size.

Use a sturdy fabric for the backing; as it's a floor cushion it's going to get some wear and tear so a thicker cotton or calico would be ideal.

INSTRUCTIONS

Front

Using A, ch126.

Row 1 (RS): 1dc in second ch from hook and in each ch to end, turn. (125 sts)

Rows 2 to 52: Now follow Bumblebee Throw patt, starting at Row 2 (using A) and finishing at end of Row 52, using A and B as indicated.

Rows 53 to 172: Rep Rows 5 to 52 of Bumblebee Throw patt twice more, then Rows 5 to 28 of Bumblebee Throw patt once more.

Row 173: Using A, ch1, 1dc, *3mtr, [1dc, 1mtr] 8 times, 1dc; rep from * to last 4 sts, 3mtr, 1dc, turn.

Row 174: Ch1, 1dc in each st to end.

Fasten off and weave in ends.

EDGING

Round 1 (RS): Join C with a slst in top right hand st on edge of Front, ch1 (does not count as st throughout), (1dc, ch2, 1dc) in same st, 1dc in each st to last st on top edge, (1dc, ch2, 1dc) in last st, rotate work 90 degrees, 1dc in each of next three row ends *skip next row end, 1dc in each of next four row ends; rep from * to end of this side, finishing on any st in rep, rotate work, (1dc, ch2, 1dc) in first st on bottom edge, 1dc in each st to last st on bottom edge, (1dc, ch2, 1dc) in last st, rotate work, 1dc in each of next three row ends, **skip next row end, 1dc in each of next four row ends; rep from ** to end of last side, finishing on any st in rep, slst to beg dc, turn.

Round 2 (WS): Ch1, *1dc in each st to 2ch-sp, (1dc, ch2, 1dc) in ch-sp; rep from * around to end, slst to beg dc.

Add more rounds of dc edging in C if you need to make your cover slightly larger.

Fasten off and weave in all ends.

ASSEMBLY

With WS facing, fold in and iron a seam of 1cm (⅜in) around all four sides of the backing fabric (to make the square the same dimensions as the cushion pad). Lay the fabric on a flat surface, with WS and folded-in edges facing up, and place the Front on top with RS facing up. Pin together around three sides, slightly stretching the crocheted fabric to fit as necessary. With needle and thread, carefully sew tiny running stitches around three edges, passing the needle through both crochet and backing fabric, approx. 3mm (⅛in) from the outside edge. Insert the cushion pad, then sew up the final side in the same way to finish.

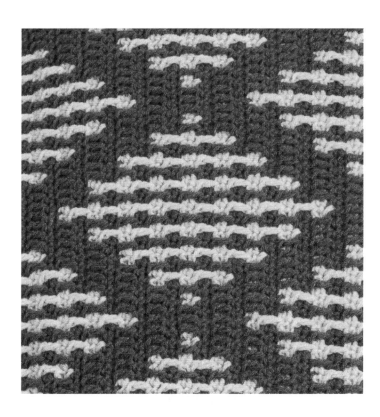

TOP TIP

If this cushion is too large for your living space, calculate a shorter starting chain and make a few scatter cushions for comfy lounging instead.

Diamonds Throw

Another design featuring diamonds, because I just can't get enough of their simple beauty and marvellous tessellating qualities. This one reminds me of a flock of geese flying overhead in formation. I don't know why, but the sound of the geese honking as they fly over my house to the river always makes me rush outside to watch them. It's better than TV. The black and off-white colour scheme of this throw works so well and, with the bright green border at each end, this diamondy design is both modern and hypnotic.

YOU WILL NEED

YARN

Scheepjes Colour Crafter (100% Acrylic), DK/light worsted, 100g (300m/328yd), in the following shades:

Malmédy (2014); 2 balls (A)

Verviers (2017); 3 balls (B)

Ede (1002); 3 balls (C)

HOOK

5.5mm crochet hook

OTHER TOOLS

65mm (2½in) pompom maker

PATTERN MULTIPLES

Pattern works to a multiple of 22 stitches + 6 stitches for the starting chain.

TENSION (GAUGE)

14 sts and 19 rows measure 10 x 10cm (4 x 4in) over patt using a 5.5mm hook.

FINISHED SIZE

Approx. 98cm x 121cm (38½ x 47½in)

Note

This throw starts with 14 foundation rows in A before the main pattern is worked in B and C. At the end, another 14 rows of A finish off the design. A big pompom in A is sewn onto each corner. A great starter pattern, as every fourth row of the main pattern is just a row of double crochet.

INSTRUCTIONS

Using A, ch138.

Foundation row 1 (RS): 1dc in second ch from hook and in each ch to end, turn. (137 sts)

Foundation rows 2 to 14: Ch1 (does not count as st throughout), 1dc in each st to end, turn. Cc to B at end of Row 14, fasten off A.

Main pattern

Row 1 (RS): Using B, ch1 (does not count as st throughout), 1dc in each st to end, turn. (137 sts)

Row 2 (WS): Ch1, 1dc in each st to end, cc to C, turn.

Row 3: Ch1, 1dc, ch2, skip 1 st, 1dc, *ch4, skip 3 sts, 5dc, ch6, skip 5 sts, 5dc, ch4, skip 3 sts, 1dc; rep from * to last 2 sts, ch2, skip 1 st, 1dc, turn.

Row 4: Ch1, 1dc, ch2, skip 2ch-sp, 1dc, *ch4, skip 4ch-sp, 5dc, ch6, skip 6ch-sp, 5dc, ch4, skip 4ch-sp, 1dc; rep from * to last 2 sts, ch2, skip 2ch-sp, 1dc, cc to B, turn.

Row 5: Ch1, 1dc, 1mtr, 1dc, *3mtr, 5dc, 5mtr, 5dc, 3mtr, 1dc; rep from * to last 2 sts, 1mtr, 1dc, turn.

Row 6: As Row 2.

Row 7: Ch1, 1dc, ch2, skip 1 st, 2dc, [ch4, skip 3 sts, 5dc] twice, ch4, skip 3 sts, *3dc, [ch4, skip 3 sts, 5dc] twice, ch4, skip 3 sts; rep from * to last 4 sts, 2dc, ch2, skip 1 st, 1dc, turn.

Row 8: Ch1, 1dc, ch2, skip 2ch-sp, 2dc, [ch4, skip 4ch-sp, 5dc] twice, ch4, skip 4ch-sp, *3dc, [ch4, skip 4ch-sp, 5dc] twice, ch4, skip 4ch-sp; rep from * to last 4 sts, 2dc, ch2, skip 2ch-sp, 1dc, cc, turn.

Row 9: Ch1, 1dc, 1mtr, 2dc, [3mtr, 5dc] twice, 3mtr, *3dc, [3mtr, 5dc] twice, 3mtr; rep from * to last 4 sts, 2dc, 1mtr, 1dc, turn.

Row 10: As Row 2.

Row 11: Ch1, 1dc, ch2, skip 1 st, 3dc, ch4, skip 3 sts, 5dc, ch2, skip 1 st, 5dc, ch4, skip 3 sts, *5dc, ch4, skip 3 sts, 5dc, ch2, skip 1 st, 5dc, ch4, skip 3 sts; rep from * to last 5 sts, 3dc, ch2, skip 1 st, 1dc, turn.

Row 12: Ch1, 1dc, ch2, skip 2ch-sp, 3dc, ch4, skip 4ch-sp, 5dc, ch2, skip 2ch-sp, 5dc, ch4, skip 4ch-sp, *5dc, ch4, skip 4ch-sp, 5dc, ch2, skip 2ch-sp, 5dc, ch4, skip 4ch-sp; rep from * to last 5 sts, 3dc, ch2, skip 2ch-sp, 1dc, cc, turn.

Row 13: Ch1, 1dc, 1mtr, 3dc, 3mtr, 5dc, 1mtr, 5dc, 3mtr, *5dc, 3mtr, 5dc, 1mtr, 5dc, 3mtr; rep from * to last 5 sts, 3dc, 1mtr, 1dc, turn.

Row 14: As Row 2.

Row 15: Ch1, 1dc, ch2, skip 1 st, 4dc, ch4, skip 3 sts, 9dc, ch4, skip 3 sts, *7dc, ch4, skip 3 sts, 9dc, ch4, skip 3 sts; rep from * to last 6 sts, 4dc, ch2, skip 1 st, 1dc, turn.

Row 16: Ch1, 1dc, ch2, skip 2ch-sp, 4dc, ch4, skip 4ch-sp, 9dc, ch4, skip 4ch-sp, *7dc, ch4, skip 4ch-sp, 9dc, ch4, skip 4ch-sp; rep from * to last 6 sts, 4dc, ch2, skip 2ch-sp, 1dc, cc, turn.

Row 17: Ch1, 1dc, 1mtr, 4dc, 3mtr, 9dc, 3mtr, *7dc, 3mtr, 9dc, 3mtr; rep from * to last 6 sts, 4dc, 1mtr, 1dc, turn.

Row 18: As Row 2.

Row 19: Ch1, 1dc, ch2, skip 1 st, 5dc, ch4, skip 3 sts, 7dc, ch4, skip 3 sts, *9dc, ch4, skip 3 sts, 7dc, ch4, skip 3 sts; rep from * to last 7 sts, 5dc, ch2, skip 1 st, 1dc, turn.

Row 20: Ch1, 1dc, ch2, skip 2ch-sp, 5dc, ch4, skip 4ch-sp, 7dc, ch4, skip 4ch-sp, *9dc, ch4, skip 4ch-sp, 7dc, ch4, skip 4ch-sp; rep from * to last 7 sts, 5dc, ch2, skip 2ch-sp, 1dc, cc, turn.

Row 21: Ch1, 1dc, 1mtr, 5dc, 3mtr, 7dc, 3mtr, *9dc, 3mtr, 7dc, 3mtr; rep from * to last 7 sts, 5dc, 1mtr, 1dc, turn.

Row 22: As Row 2.

Row 23: Ch1, 1dc, ch3, skip 2 sts, [5dc, ch4, skip 3 sts] twice, *5dc, ch2, skip 1 st, [5dc, ch4, skip 3 sts] twice; rep from * to last 8 sts, 5dc, ch3, skip 2 sts, 1dc, turn.

Row 24: Ch1, 1dc, ch3, skip 3ch-sp, [5dc, ch4, skip 4ch-sp] twice, *5dc, ch2, skip 2ch-sp, [5dc, ch4, skip 4ch-sp] twice; rep from * to last 8 sts, 5dc, ch3, skip 3ch-sp, 1dc, cc, turn.

Row 25: Ch1, 1dc, 2mtr, [5dc, 3mtr] twice, *5dc, 1mtr, [5dc, 3mtr] twice; rep from * to last 8 sts, 5dc, 2mtr, 1dc, turn.

Row 26: As Row 2.

Row 27: Ch1, 1dc, ch4, skip 3 sts, 5dc, ch4, skip 3 sts, 3dc, ch4, skip 3 sts, * [5dc, ch4, skip 3 sts] twice, 3dc, ch4, skip 3 sts; rep from * to last 9 sts, 5dc, ch4, skip 3 sts, 1dc, turn.

Row 28: Ch1, 1dc, ch4, skip 4ch-sp, 5dc, ch4, skip 4ch-sp, 3dc, ch4, skip 4ch-sp, *[5dc, ch4, skip 4ch-sp] twice, 3dc, ch4, skip 4ch-sp; rep from * to last 9 sts, 5dc, ch4, skip 4ch-sp, 1dc, cc, turn.

Row 29: Ch1, 1dc, 3mtr, 5dc, 3mtr, 3dc, 3mtr, *[5dc, 3mtr] twice, 3dc, 3mtr; rep from * to last 9 sts, 5dc, 3mtr, 1dc, turn.

Row 30: As Row 2.

Row 31: Ch1, 1dc, ch5, skip 4 sts, 5dc, ch4, skip 3 sts, 1dc, ch4, skip 3 sts, *5dc, ch6, skip 5 sts, 5dc, ch4, skip 3 sts, 1dc, ch4, skip 3 sts; rep from * to last 10 sts, 5dc, ch5, skip 4 sts, 1dc, turn.

Row 32: Ch1, 1dc, ch5, skip 5ch-sp, 5dc, ch4, skip 4ch-sp, 1dc, ch4, skip 4ch-sp, *5dc, ch6, skip 6ch-sp, 5dc, ch4, skip 4ch-sp, 1dc, ch4, skip 4ch-sp; rep from * to last 10 sts, 5dc, ch5, skip 5ch-sp, 1dc, cc, turn.

Row 33: Ch1, 1dc, 4mtr, 5dc, 3mtr, 1dc, 3mtr, *5dc, 5mtr, 5dc, 3mtr, 1dc, 3mtr; rep from * to last 10 sts, 5dc, 4mtr, 1dc, turn.

Row 34: As Row 2.

Row 35: Ch1, 1dc, ch4, skip 3 sts, 5dc, ch4, skip 3 sts, 3dc, ch4, skip 3 sts, * [5dc, ch4, skip 3 sts] twice, 3dc, ch4, skip 3 sts; rep from * to last 9 sts, 5dc, ch4, skip 3 sts, 1dc, turn.

Row 36: Ch1, 1dc, ch4, skip 4ch-sp, 5dc, ch4, skip 4ch-sp, 3dc, ch4, skip 4ch-sp, *[5dc, ch4, skip 4ch-sp] twice, 3dc, ch4, skip 4ch-sp; rep from * to last 9 sts, 5dc, ch4, skip 4ch-sp, 1dc, cc, turn.

Row 37: Ch1, 1dc, 3mtr, 5dc, 3mtr, 3dc, 3mtr, *[5dc, 3mtr] twice, 3dc, 3mtr; rep from * to last 9 sts, 5dc, 3mtr, 1dc, turn.

Row 38: As Row 2.

Row 39: Ch1, 1dc, ch3, skip 2 sts, [5dc, ch4, skip 3 sts] twice, *5dc, ch2, skip 1 st, [5dc, ch4, skip 3 sts] twice; rep from * to last 8 sts, 5dc, ch3, skip 2 sts, 1dc, turn.

Row 40: Ch1, 1dc, ch3, skip 3ch-sp, [5dc, ch4, skip 4ch-sp] twice, *5dc, ch2, skip 2ch-sp, [5dc, ch4, skip 4ch-sp] twice; rep from * to last 8 sts, 5dc, ch3, skip 3ch-sp, 1dc, cc, turn.

Row 41: Ch1, 1dc, 2mtr, [5dc, 3mtr] twice, *5dc, 1mtr, [5dc, 3mtr] twice; rep from * to last 8 sts, 5dc, 2mtr, 1dc, turn.

Row 42: As Row 2.

Row 43: Ch1, 1dc, ch2, skip 1 st, 5dc, ch4, skip 3 sts, 7dc, ch4, skip 3 sts, *9dc, ch4, skip 3 sts, 7dc, ch4, skip 3 sts; rep from * to last 7 sts, 5dc, ch2, skip 1 st, 1dc, turn.

Row 44: Ch1, 1dc, ch2, skip 2ch-sp, 5dc, ch4, skip 4ch-sp, 7dc, ch4, skip 4ch-sp, *9dc, ch4, skip 4ch-sp, 7dc, ch4, skip 4ch-sp; rep from * to last 7 sts, 5dc, ch2, skip 2ch-sp, 1dc, cc, turn.

Row 45: Ch1, 1dc, 1mtr, 5dc, 3mtr, 7dc, 3mtr, *9dc, 3mtr, 7dc, 3mtr; rep from * to last 7 sts, 5dc, 1mtr, 1dc, turn.

Row 46: As Row 2.

Row 47: Ch1, 1dc, ch2, skip 1 st, 4dc, ch4, skip 3 sts, 9dc, ch4, skip 3 sts, *7dc, ch4, skip 3 sts, 9dc, ch4, skip 3 sts; rep from * to last 6 sts, 4dc, ch2, skip 1 st, 1dc, turn.

Row 48: Ch1, 1dc, ch2, skip 2ch-sp, 4dc, ch4, skip 4ch-sp, 9dc, ch4, skip 4ch-sp, *7dc, ch4, skip 4ch-sp, 9dc, ch4, skip 4ch-sp; rep from * to last 6 sts, 4dc, ch2, skip 2ch-sp, 1dc, cc, turn.

Row 49: Ch1, 1dc, 1mtr, 4dc, 3mtr, 9dc, 3mtr, *7dc, 3mtr, 9dc, 3mtr; rep from * to last 6 sts, 4dc, 1mtr, 1dc, turn.

Row 50: As Row 2.

Row 51: Ch1, 1dc, ch2, skip 1 st, 3dc, ch4, skip 3 sts, 5dc, ch2, skip 1 st, 5dc, ch4, skip 3 sts, *5dc, ch4, skip 3 sts, 5dc, ch2, skip 1 st, 5dc, ch4, skip 3 sts; rep from * to last 5 sts, 3dc, ch2, skip 1 st, 1dc, turn.

Row 52: Ch1, 1dc, ch2, skip 2ch-sp, 3dc, ch4, skip 4ch-sp, 5dc, ch2, skip 2ch-sp, 5dc, ch4, skip 4ch-sp, *5dc, ch4, skip 4ch-sp, 5dc, ch2, skip 2ch-sp, 5dc, ch4, skip 4ch-sp; rep from * to last 5 sts, 3dc, ch2, skip 2ch-sp, 1dc, cc, turn.

Row 53: Ch1, 1dc, 1mtr, 3dc, 3mtr, 5dc, 1mtr, 5dc, 3mtr, *5dc, 3mtr, 5dc, 1mtr, 5dc, 3mtr; rep from * to last 5 sts, 3dc, 1mtr, 1dc, turn.

Row 54: As Row 2.

Row 55: Ch1, 1dc, ch2, skip 1 st, 2dc, [ch4, skip 3 sts, 5dc] twice, ch4, skip 3 sts, *3dc, [ch4, skip 3 sts, 5dc] twice, ch4, skip 3 sts; rep from * to last 4 sts, 2dc, ch2, skip 1 st, 1dc, turn.

Row 56: Ch1, 1dc, ch2, skip 2ch-sp, 2dc, [ch4, skip 4ch-sp, 5dc] twice, ch4, skip 4ch-sp, *3dc, [ch4, skip 4ch-sp, 5dc] twice, ch4, skip 4ch-sp; rep from * to last 4 sts, 2dc, ch2, skip 2ch-sp, 1dc, cc, turn.

Row 57: Ch1, 1dc, 1mtr, 2dc, [3mtr, 5dc] twice, 3mtr, *3dc, [3mtr, 5dc] twice, 3mtr; rep from * to last 4 sts, 2dc, 1mtr, 1dc, turn.

Row 58: As Row 2.

Rows 59 to 202: Rep Rows 3 to 58 twice more, then rep Rows 3 to 34 once more, cc to A at end of Row 202.

Fasten off B and C.

Rows 203 to 216: Using A, rep Foundation row 2 a total of 14 times.

Fasten off and weave in ends.

POMPOMS
(make 4)

Using A and pompom maker, make four pompoms. Attach one to each corner to finish and weave in all ends.

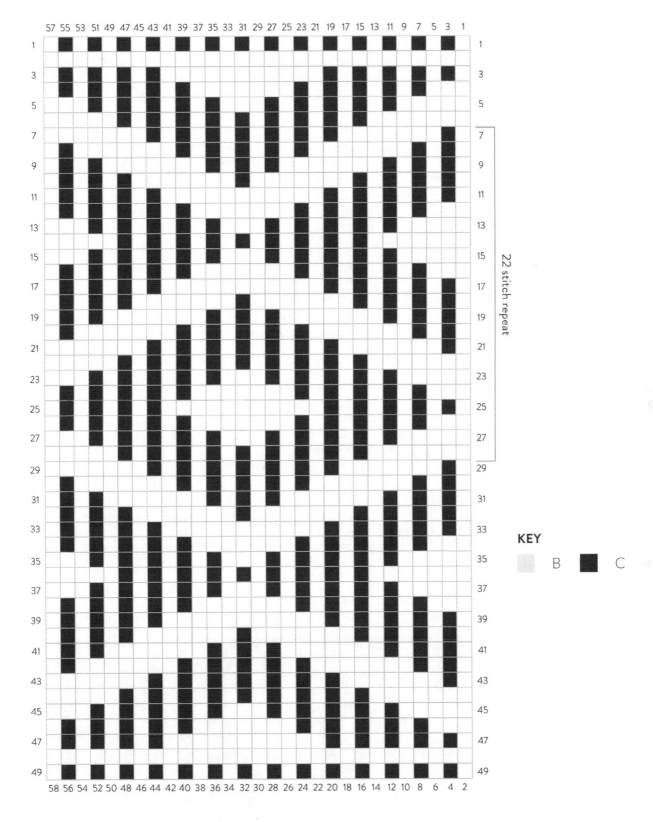

Each square represents a stitch.

To work from this chart, rotate it by 90 degrees clockwise. Read all odd-numbered (RS) rows from right to left, and all even-numbered (WS) rows from left to right.

Work 14 rows of dc in A before beginning on chart. Work rows 1 to 58 to start, and on subsequent repeats work rows 3 to 58. Finish with 14 rows of dc in A.

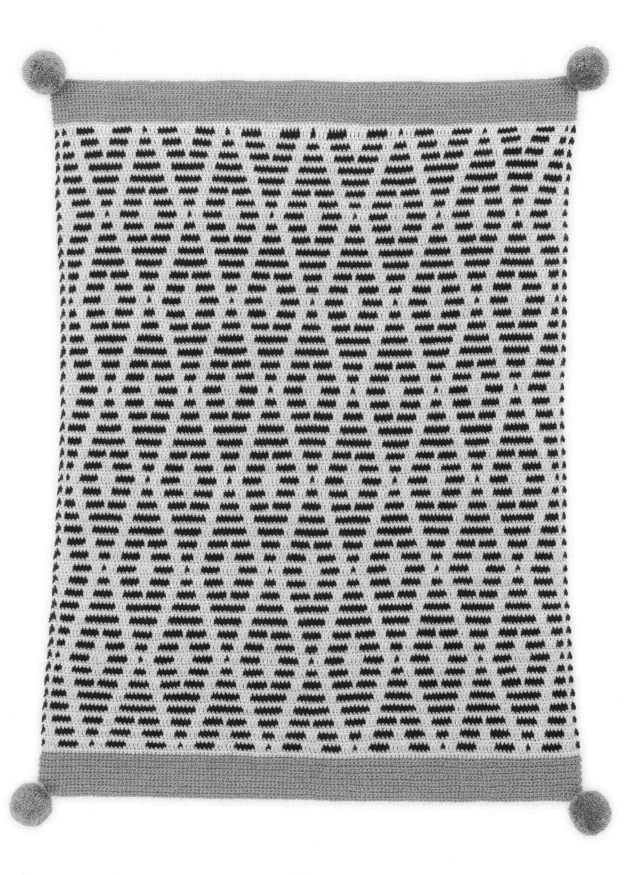

TOP TIP

A great starter project – this is an easy pattern to find your mosaic crochet rhythm.

Try a new colourway

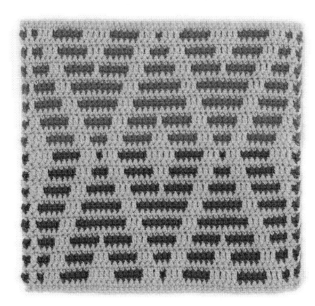

OPPOSITES ATTRACT

Going straight across the colour wheel, and delving into tertiary colours, too: coral and teal may be opposite to each other, but together they absolutely shine and complement each other perfectly.

SPIN-OFF PROJECT:
Fluffy Diamond Rug

This is a real treat of a rug. Not only is it easy to make, it looks fabulous and is super soft too, thanks to the mix of chunky and fluffy yarns. It looks lovely in any room, but mine has become a rather luxurious bathmat. My feet thank me every time they step onto its welcoming pattern instead of onto a cold floor. A hot bath followed by a fluffy rug underfoot and a massive cup of tea; absolute bliss!

YOU WILL NEED

YARN

Scheepjes Chunky Monkey (100% acrylic), aran/worsted, 100g (116m/126yds), in the following shade:

Dark Grey (2018); 5 balls (A)

Scheepjes Sweetheart Soft (100% polyester), chunky/bulky, 100g (153m/167yds), in the following shades:

Light grey (02); 3 balls (B)

Green (23); 1 ball (C)

HOOK

5mm crochet hook

PATTERN MULTIPLES

Pattern works to a multiple of 22 stitches + 6 stitches for the starting chain.

TENSION (GAUGE)

13 sts and 15 rows measure 10 x 10cm (4 x 4in) over patt using a 5mm hook.

FINISHED SIZE

Approx. 74 x 100cm (29 x 39½in)

Notes

The background is in a chunky yarn (A), whilst the diamonds and edging are both in a fluffy yarn (B and C).

Keep a careful eye on your stitch count for the rows in B and C as the fluffiness hides the stitches. It is easier to feel for the next stitch to work into with your fingers, rather than trying to find it with your eyes.

It's really important your finished rug is not a slip hazard on hard floors. My preferred method is to cut a piece of Anti Slip Rug Underlay to the same size as the rug and tack it securely onto the underside with small stitches. Alternatively, there are paint-like products that you can apply directly onto the back of the rug. I haven't used these so I can't comment on their efficacy. Whatever you use, please keep your rug safe and non-slip!

INSTRUCTIONS

Using C, ch94.

Foundation row 1 (RS): 1dc in second ch from hook and in each ch to end, turn. (93 sts)

Foundation row 2 (WS): Ch1 (does not count as st throughout), 1dc in each st to end, cc to A, fasten off C, turn.

Main pattern

Row 1 (RS): Using A, ch1, 1dc in each st to end, turn. (93 sts)

Rows 2 to 58: Now follow Diamonds Throw Main Patt, starting at Row 2 (using A) and finishing at end of Row 58, using A and B where B and C are indicated in patt.

Rows 59 to 146: Rep Rows 3 to 58 of Diamonds Throw Main Patt once more, then rep Rows 3 to 34 of Diamonds Throw Main Patt once more. Cc to C at end of Row 146.

Fasten off A and B.

Rows 147 and 148: Using C, rep Foundation row 2 twice.

Do not fasten off C.

EDGING

Edging is worked along two long sides only.

First long side

Row 1 (WS): Using C and with WS facing, ch1, rotate work 90 degrees and work along first long side as follows: *1dc in each of next four row ends, skip next row end; rep from * to end, finishing on any st in rep. If last st happens to be a skipped st, just make 1dc to finish row. Turn.

Row 2 (RS): Ch1, 1dc in each st to end.

Fasten off and weave in ends.

Second long side

Row 1 (WS): With WS facing, join C with a slst in first row end on other long side, ch1, 1dc in same st, 1dc in each of next three row ends, *skip next row end, 1dc in each of next four row ends; rep from * to end, finishing on any st in rep. If last st happens to be a skipped st, just make 1dc to finish row. Turn.

Row 2 (RS): Ch1, 1dc in each st to end, turn.

Fasten off and weave in ends.

TOP TIP

This would make a fabulous hallway runner in a chunky cotton yarn.

Cool as Flock Throw

SKILL LEVEL:

It was always high excitement to visit my grandparents when I was little. They lived in London, and the thrill of riding on a double decker bus through the East End was almost too much for a country girl like me. My grandparents were kind and loving; they taught me how to play cards and how to always find space for second helpings of pudding. They also had the most fabulous swirly flock wallpaper in every room; I remember running my fingers over it because I loved the texture and patterns. This one is in honour of my grandparents, Rosa and Ken, with love.

YOU WILL NEED

YARN

Scheepjes Namaste (50% virgin wool/50% acrylic), chunky/bulky 100g (85m/93yds), in the following shades:

Upward Salute (630); 7 balls (A)

Peacock (609); 7 balls (B)

HOOK

8mm crochet hook

PATTERN MULTIPLES

Pattern works to a multiple of 12 stitches + 4 stitches for the starting chain.

TENSION (GAUGE)

10 sts and 14 rows measure 10 x 10cm (4 x 4in) over patt using an 8mm hook.

FINISHED SIZE

Approx. 87 x 113cm (34¼ x 44½in)

Note

Once the main throw is made, the two long sides are edged in A, then a tassel is attached to each corner.

INSTRUCTIONS

Using A, ch88.

Row 1 (RS): 1dc in second ch from hook and in each ch to end, turn. (87 sts)

Row 2 (WS): Ch1 (does not count as st throughout), 1dc in each st to end, cc to B, turn.

Row 3: Ch1, 1dc, ch2, skip 1 st, 1dc, *ch2, skip 1 st, 3dc; rep from * to last 4 sts, [ch2, skip 1 st, 1dc] twice, turn.

Row 4: Ch1, 1dc, ch2, skip 2ch-sp, 1dc, *ch2, skip 2ch-sp, 3dc; rep from * to last 4 sts, [ch2, skip 2ch-sp, 1dc] twice, cc to A, turn.

Row 5: Ch1, [1dc, 1mtr] twice, ch2, skip 1 st, 2dc, 1mtr, 2dc, ch2, skip 1 st, *1mtr, 3dc, 1mtr, ch2, skip 1 st, 2dc, 1mtr, 2dc, ch2, skip 1 st; rep from * to last 4 sts, [1mtr, 1dc] twice, turn.

Row 6: Ch1, 4dc, ch2, skip 2ch-sp, *5dc, ch2, skip 2ch-sp; rep from * to last 4 sts, 4dc, cc, turn.

Row 7: Ch1, 1dc, *ch2, skip 1 st, 2dc, 1mtr, ch2, skip 1 st, 3dc, ch2, skip 1 st, 1mtr, 2dc; rep from * to last 2 sts, ch2, skip 1 st, 1dc, turn.

Row 8: Ch1, 1dc, *ch2, skip 2ch-sp, 3dc; rep from * to last 2 sts, ch2, skip 2ch-sp, 1dc, cc, turn.

Row 9: Ch1, 1dc, 1mtr, *ch2, skip 1 st, 2dc, 1mtr, ch4, skip 3 sts, 1mtr, 2dc, ch2, skip 1 st, 1mtr; rep from * to last st, 1dc, turn.

Row 10: Ch1, 2dc, *ch2, skip 2ch-sp, 3dc, ch4, skip 4ch-sp, 3dc, ch2, skip 2ch-sp, 1dc; rep from * to last st, 1dc, cc, turn.

Row 11: Ch1, 1dc, ch2, skip 1 st, 1mtr, ch2, skip 1 st, 2dc, 3mtr, 2dc, ch2, skip 1 st, 1mtr, *1dc, 1mtr, ch2, skip 1 st, 2dc, 3mtr, 2dc, ch2, skip 1 st, 1mtr; rep from * to last 2 sts, ch2, skip 1 st, 1dc, turn.

Row 12: Ch1, [1dc, ch2, skip 2ch-sp] twice, 7dc, *ch2, skip 2ch-sp, 3dc, ch2, skip 2ch-sp, 7dc; rep from * to last 4 sts, [ch2, skip 2ch-sp, 1dc] twice, cc, turn.

Row 13: Ch1, [1dc, 1mtr] twice, ch4, skip 3 sts, 1dc, ch4, skip 3 sts, 1mtr, *3dc, 1mtr, ch4, skip 3 sts, 1dc, ch4, skip 3 sts, 1mtr; rep from * to last 3 sts, 1dc, 1mtr, 1dc, turn.

Row 14: Ch1, 4dc, ch4, skip 4ch-sp, 1dc, ch4, skip 4ch-sp, *5dc, ch4, skip 4ch-sp, 1dc, ch4, skip 4ch-sp; rep from * to last 4 sts, 4dc, cc, turn.

Row 15: Ch1, [1dc, ch2, skip 1 st] twice, 3mtr, 1dc, 3mtr, *ch2, skip 1 st, 3dc, ch2, skip 1 st, 3mtr, 1dc, 3mtr; rep from * to last 4 sts, [ch2, skip 1 st, 1dc] twice, turn.

Row 16: Ch1, [1dc, ch2, skip 2ch-sp] twice, 7dc, *ch2, skip 2ch-sp, 3dc, ch2, skip 2ch-sp, 7dc; rep from * to last 4 sts, [ch2, skip 2ch-sp, 1dc] twice, cc, turn.

Row 17: Ch1, 1dc, 1mtr, ch2, skip 1 st, 1mtr, 2dc, ch4, skip 3 sts, 2dc, 1mtr, ch2, skip 1 st, *1dc, ch2, skip 1 st, 1mtr, 2dc, ch4, skip 3 sts, 2dc, 1mtr, ch2, skip 1 st; rep from * to last 2 sts, 1mtr, 1dc, turn.

Row 18: Ch1, 2dc, *ch2, skip 2ch-sp, 3dc, ch4, skip 4ch-sp, 3dc, ch2, skip 2ch-sp, 1dc; rep from * to last st, 1dc, cc, turn.

Row 19: Ch1, 1dc, *ch2, skip 1 st, 1mtr, 2dc, ch2, skip 1 st, 3mtr, ch2, skip 1 st, 2dc, 1mtr; rep from * to last 2 sts, ch2, skip 1 st, 1dc, turn.

Row 20: Ch1, 1dc, *ch2, skip 2ch-sp, 3dc; rep from * to last 2 sts, ch2, skip 2ch-sp, 1dc, cc, turn.

Row 21: Ch1, 1dc, 1mtr, 2dc, ch2, skip 1 st, 1mtr, 3dc, 1mtr, ch2, skip 1 st, *2dc, 1mtr, 2dc, ch2, skip 1 st, 1mtr, 3dc, 1mtr, ch2, skip 1 st; rep from * to last 4 sts, 2dc, 1mtr, 1dc, turn.

Row 22: Ch1, 4dc, ch2, skip 2ch-sp, *5dc, ch2, skip 2ch-sp; rep from * to last 4 sts, 4dc, cc, turn.

Row 23: Ch1, [1dc, ch2, skip 1 st] twice, 1mtr, 2dc, ch2, skip 1 st, 2dc, 1mtr, *ch2, skip 1 st, 3dc, ch2, skip 1 st, 1mtr, 2dc, ch2, skip 1 st, 2dc, 1mtr; rep from * to last 4 sts [ch2, skip 1 st, 1dc] twice, turn.

Row 24: Ch1, 1dc, ch2, skip 2ch-sp, 1dc, *ch2, skip 2ch-sp, 3dc; rep from * to last 4 sts, [ch2, skip 2ch-sp, 1dc] twice, cc, turn.

Row 25: Ch1, 1dc, 1mtr, ch2, skip 1 st, 1mtr, 2dc, ch2, skip 1 st, 1mtr, ch2, skip 1 st, 2dc, 1mtr, *ch4, skip 3 sts, 1mtr, 2dc, ch2, skip 1 st, 1mtr, ch2, skip 1 st, 2dc, 1mtr; rep from * to last 3 sts, ch2, skip 1 st, 1mtr, 1dc, turn.

Row 26: Ch1, 2dc, ch2, skip 2ch-sp, 3dc, ch2, skip 2ch-sp, 1dc, ch2, skip 2ch-sp, 3dc, *ch4, skip 4ch-sp, 3dc, ch2, skip 2ch-sp, 1dc, ch2, skip 2ch-sp, 3dc; rep from * to last 3 sts, ch2, skip 2ch-sp, 2dc, cc, turn.

Row 27: Ch1, 1dc, ch2, skip 1 st, 1mtr, 2dc, ch2, skip 1 st, 1mtr, 1dc, 1mtr, ch2, skip 1 st, 2dc, *3mtr, 2dc, ch2, skip 1 st, 1mtr, 1dc, 1mtr, ch2, skip 1 st, 2dc; rep from * to last 3 sts, 1mtr, ch2, skip 1 st, 1dc, turn.

Row 28: Ch1, 1dc, ch2, skip 2ch-sp, [3dc, ch2, skip 2ch-sp] twice, *7dc, ch2, skip 2ch-sp, 3dc, ch2, skip 2ch-sp; rep from * to last 5 sts, 3dc, ch2, skip 2ch-sp, 1dc, cc, turn.

Row 29: Ch1, 1dc, 1mtr, ch4, skip 3 sts, 1mtr, 3dc, 1mtr, *ch4, skip 3 sts, 1dc, ch4, skip 3 sts, 1mtr, 3dc, 1mtr; rep from * to last 5 sts, ch4, skip 3 sts, 1mtr, 1dc, turn.

Row 30: Ch1, 2dc, ch4, skip 4ch-sp, 5dc, *ch4, skip 4ch-sp, 1dc, ch4, skip 4ch-sp, 5dc; rep from * to last 5 sts, ch4, skip 4ch-sp, 2dc, cc, turn.

Row 31: Ch1, 1dc, ch2, skip 1 st, 3mtr, ch2, skip 1 st, 3dc, ch2, skip 1 st, *3mtr, 1dc, 3mtr, ch2, skip 1 st, 3dc, ch2, skip 1 st; rep from * to last 5 sts, 3mtr, ch2, skip 1 st, 1dc, turn.

Row 32: Ch1, 1dc, ch2, skip 2ch-sp, [3dc, ch2, skip 2ch-sp] twice, *7dc, ch2, skip 2ch-sp, 3dc, ch2, skip 2ch-sp; rep from * to last 5 sts, 3dc, ch2, skip 2ch-sp, 1dc, cc, turn.

Row 33: Ch1, 1dc, 1mtr, ch2, skip 1 st, 2dc, 1mtr, ch2, skip 1 st, 1dc, ch2, skip 1 st, 1mtr, 2dc, *ch4, skip 3 sts, 2dc, 1mtr, ch2, skip 1 st, 1dc, ch2, skip 1 st, 1mtr, 2dc; rep from * to last 3 sts, ch2, skip 1 st, 1mtr, 1dc, turn.

Row 34: Ch1, 2dc, ch2, skip 2ch-sp, 3dc, ch2, skip 2ch-sp, 1dc, ch2, skip 2ch-sp, 3dc, *ch4, skip 4ch-sp, 3dc, ch2, skip 2ch-sp, 1dc, ch2, skip 2ch-sp, 3dc; rep from * to last 3 sts, ch2, skip 2ch-sp, 2dc, cc, turn.

Row 35: Ch1, 1dc, ch2, skip 1 st, 1mtr, ch2, skip 1 st, 2dc, 1mtr, ch2, skip 1 st, 1mtr, 2dc, ch2, skip 1 st, * 3mtr, ch2, skip 1 st, 2dc, 1mtr, ch2, skip 1 st, 1mtr, 2dc, ch2, skip 1 st; rep from * to last 3 sts, 1mtr, ch2, skip 1 st, 1dc, turn.

Row 36: Ch1, 1dc, ch2, skip 2ch-sp, 1dc, *ch2, skip 2ch-sp, 3dc; rep from * to last 4 sts, [ch2, skip 2ch-sp, 1dc] twice, cc, turn.

Rows 37 to 152: Rep Rows 5 to 36 a further 3 times, then rep Rows 5 to 24 once more.

Row 153: Ch1, [1dc, 1mtr] twice, *3dc, 1mtr; rep from * to last 3 sts, 1dc, 1mtr, 1dc, turn.

Row 154: Ch1, 1dc in each st to end.

Fasten off B and weave in end, do not fasten off A.

EDGING

Edging is worked along two long sides only.

First long side

Row 1 (WS): Using A and with WS facing, ch1, rotate work 90 degrees and work along first long side as follows: *1dc in each of next four row ends, skip next row end; rep from * to end, finishing on any st in rep. If last st happens to be a skipped st, just make 1dc to finish row. Turn.

Row 2 (RS): Ch1, 1dc in each st to end, fasten off, weave in ends.

Second long side

Row 1 (WS): With WS facing, join A with a slst in first row end on other long side, ch1, 1dc in same st, 1dc in each of next three row ends, *skip next row end, 1dc in each of next four row ends; rep from * to end, finishing on any st in rep. If last st happens to be a skipped st, just make 1dc to finish row. Turn.

Row 2 (RS): Ch1, 1dc in each st to end, turn.

Fasten off and weave in ends.

TASSELS
(make 4)

Wrap A about 22 times around a piece of card approx. 15cm (6in) in length. Insert a 30cm (12in) length of A under all the loops at the top, knot tightly to fasten and secure the loops together. Cut through all the loops along the bottom edge. Tie another 30cm (12in) piece of A around all the strands (except the joining yarn at the top) approx. 4cm (1½in) from the top. Trim tassel to level off.

Attach one tassel to each corner of the Throw, using the joining yarn at the top to knot securely to each corner.

Weave in all ends to finish.

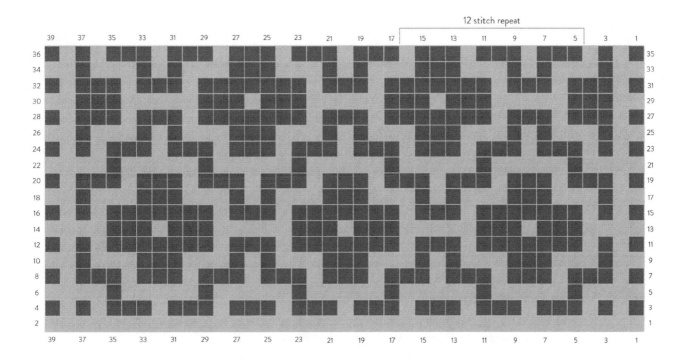

KEY

▨ A   ▦ B

Each square represents a stitch.

Read all odd-numbered (RS) rows from right to left, and all even-numbered (WS) rows from left to right.

Work rows 1 to 36 to start, and on subsequent repeats work rows 5 to 36.

TOP TIP

Luxurious chunky yarn and a large hook make this a quick and delightfully squishy make.

Try a new colourway

DEEPLY MYSTERIOUS

There's no reason that two darker tones can't make an impact together; think dark winter nights, flickering candlelight and Gothic horror stories. Here a deep pine-green holds its own very nicely with a deep jade. Spooky!

SPIN-OFF PROJECT:
Matching-Not-Matching Cushions

Reverse it up with this 'pair' of cushions. Same design, same yarns… but by switching the colours around a completely different effect is made! I adore this combination of vivid orange and soft stone-grey, but I have a feeling these cushions would look beautiful in any colours you choose.

YOU WILL NEED

YARN

Scheepjes Catona (100% cotton), 4-ply/sport, 50g (125m/136yds), in the following shades:

Champagne (248); 3 balls (A)

Royal Orange (189); 3 balls (B)

HOOK

3mm crochet hook

OTHER TOOLS AND MATERIALS

Two 35cm (13¾in) square cushion pads

Two 37cm (14½in) squares of backing fabric

Needle, threads and pins

PATTERN MULTIPLES

Pattern works to a multiple of 12 stitches + 4 stitches for the starting chain.

TENSION (GAUGE)

18 sts and 24 rows measure 10 x 10cm (4 x 4in) over patt using a 3mm hook.

FINISHED SIZE

Front measures approx. 34 x 34cm (13¼ x 13¼in)

Cushions measure 35 x 35cm (13¾ x 13¾in) once assembled

Notes

These two cushions are made of a crocheted front and a fabric backing, which are sewn together with a cushion pad inserted at the end. The crocheted covers should measure slightly smaller than the finished cushion dimensions, as you want them to stretch a little to keep their shape.

Use A and B as indicated to make the first cushion, then switch them around for the second one, using A where B is indicated, and vice versa.

INSTRUCTIONS

Front

Using A, ch64.

Row 1 (RS): 1dc in second ch from hook and in each ch to end, turn. (63 sts)

Rows 2 to 36: Now follow Cool As Flock Throw patt, starting at Row 2 (using A) and finishing at end of Row 36, using A and B as indicated.

Rows 37 to 88: Rep Rows 5 to 36 once more, then rep Rows 5 to 24 once more.

Row 89: Using A, ch1, [1dc, 1mtr] twice, *3dc, 1mtr; rep from * to last 3 sts, 1dc, 1mtr, 1dc, turn.

Row 90: Ch1, 1dc in each st to end.

Fasten off B, do not fasten off A.

EDGING

Edge two side row-end edges in A using same method as for Cool As Flock Throw.

Fasten off and weave in ends.

Make the second Front in the same way, using B where A is indicated, and A where B is indicated for the other colourway.

ASSEMBLY

With WS facing, fold in and iron a seam of 1cm (⅜in) around all four sides of the backing fabric (to make a square to the same dimensions as the cushion pad). Lay the fabric on a flat surface, with WS and folded-in edges facing up, and place the Front on top with RS facing up. Pin them together around three sides, slightly stretching the crocheted fabric to fit as necessary. With a needle and thread, carefully sew tiny running stitches around the three edges, passing the needle through both crochet and backing fabric approx. 3mm (⅛in) from the outside edge. Insert the cushion pad, and sew up the final side in the same way to finish.

TOP TIP

If the crocheted covers come up a bit too small, just work some extra rounds of double crochet around the edge to make a stylish, chunky border.

Misty Mountains Throw

This throw taught me a valuable lesson: never ever rule out a colour until you've tried it! I had no idea that pale pink (not my favourite colour in the world…) would work so well with this lovely gold-orange, but once the pattern started to emerge, the colours looked totally gorgeous together. This design pays homage to my first-ever mosaic crochet pattern from a few years ago, the Diamond Heart Throw. This time round though it gets a 'half-diamond' twist, which turns the design into these beautiful 'reflected' mountain peaks. And yes, the name… one for all you Tolkien fans out there… my Other Half and my son begged me to name this one Misty Mountains. So I did.

YOU WILL NEED

YARN

Scheepjes Colour Crafter (100% Acrylic), DK/light worsted, 100g (300m/328yds), in the following shades:

Burum (1709); 5 balls (A)

Ommen (1240); 3 balls (B)

HOOK

5.5mm crochet hook

OTHER TOOLS

65mm (2½in) pompom maker

PATTERN MULTIPLES

Pattern works to a multiple of 20 stitches + 6 stitches for the starting chain.

TENSION (GAUGE)

14 sts and 18 rows measure 10 x 10cm (4 x 4in) over patt using a 5.5mm hook.

FINISHED SIZE

Approx. 105 x 135cm (41¼ x 53¼in)

Note

Yarn A is used for the background colour and B makes the pale pink mountains. This is a good starter pattern, as every fourth row is just a row of double crochet. Once the main throw is made, it is finished with a simple edging in B and a pompom on each corner.

INSTRUCTIONS

Using A, ch146.

Row 1 (RS): 1dc in second ch from hook and in each ch to end, turn. (145 sts)

Row 2 (WS): Ch1 (does not count as st throughout), 1dc in each st to end, cc to B, turn.

Row 3: Ch1, 1dc, ch3, skip 2 sts, 5dc, ch10, skip 9 sts, 5dc, *ch2, skip 1 st, 5dc, ch10, skip 9 sts, 5dc; rep from * to last 3 sts, ch3, skip 2 sts, 1dc, turn.

Row 4: Ch1, 1dc, ch3, skip 3ch-sp, 5dc, ch10, skip 10ch-sp, 5dc, *ch2, skip 2ch-sp, 5dc, ch10, skip 10ch-sp, 5dc; rep from * to last 3 sts, ch3, skip 3ch-sp, 1dc, cc to A, turn.

Row 5: Ch1, 1dc, 2mtr, 5dc, 9mtr, 5dc, *1mtr, 5dc, 9mtr, 5dc; rep from * to last 3 sts, 2mtr, 1dc, turn.

Row 6: As Row 2.

Row 7: Ch1, 1dc, *ch4, skip 3 sts, 5dc, ch8, skip 7 sts, 5dc; rep from * to last 4 sts, ch4, skip 3 sts, 1dc, turn.

Row 8: Ch1, 1dc, *ch4, skip 4ch-sp, 5dc, ch8, skip 8ch-sp, 5dc; rep from * to last 4 sts, ch4, skip 4ch-sp, 1dc, cc, turn.

Row 9: Ch1, 1dc, *3mtr, 5dc, 7mtr, 5dc; rep from * to last 4 sts, 3mtr, 1dc, turn.

Row 10: As Row 2.

Row 11: Ch1, 1dc, ch5, skip 4 sts, 5dc, *ch6, skip 5 sts, 5dc; rep from * to last 5 sts, ch5, skip 4 sts, 1dc, turn.

Row 12: Ch1, 1dc, ch5, skip 5ch-sp, 5dc, *ch6, skip 6ch-sp, 5dc; rep from * to last 5 sts, ch5, skip 5ch-sp, 1dc, cc, turn.

Row 13: Ch1, 1dc, 4mtr, 5dc, *5mtr, 5dc; rep from * to last 5 sts, 4mtr, 1dc, turn.

Row 14: As Row 2.

Row 15: Ch1, 1dc, ch6, skip 5 sts, 5dc, ch4, skip 3 sts, 5dc, *ch8, skip 7 sts, 5dc, ch4, skip 3 sts, 5dc; rep from * to last 6 sts, ch6, skip 5 sts, 1dc, turn.

Row 16: Ch1, 1dc, ch6, skip 6ch-sp, 5dc, ch4, skip 4ch-sp, 5dc, *ch8, skip 8ch-sp, 5dc, ch4, skip 4ch-sp, 5dc; rep from * to last 6 sts, ch6, skip 6ch-sp, 1dc, cc, turn.

Row 17: Ch1, 1dc, 5mtr, 5dc, 3mtr, 5dc, *7mtr, 5dc, 3mtr, 5dc; rep from * to last 6 sts, 5mtr, 1dc, turn.

Row 18: As Row 2.

Row 19: Ch1, 1dc, ch7, skip 6 sts, 5dc, ch2, skip 1 st, 5dc, *ch10, skip 9 sts, 5dc, ch2, skip 1 st, 5dc; rep from * to last 7 sts, ch7, skip 6 sts, 1dc, turn.

Row 20: Ch1, 1dc, ch7, skip 7ch-sp, 5dc, ch2, skip 2ch-sp, 5dc, *ch10, skip 10ch-sp, 5dc, ch2, skip 2ch-sp, 5dc; rep from * to last 7 sts, ch7, skip 7ch-sp, 1dc, cc, turn.

Row 21: Ch1, 1dc, 6mtr, 5dc, 1mtr, 5dc, *9mtr, 5dc, 1mtr, 5dc; rep from * to last 7 sts, 6mtr, 1dc, turn.

Row 22: As Row 2.

Row 23: Ch1, 1dc, ch2, skip 1 st, *1dc, ch6, skip 5 sts, 9dc, ch6, skip 5 sts; rep from * to last 3 sts, 1dc, ch2, skip 1 st, 1dc, turn.

Row 24: Ch1, 1dc, ch2, skip 2ch-sp, *1dc, ch6, skip 6ch-sp, 9dc, ch6, skip 6ch-sp; rep from * to last 3 sts, 1dc, ch2, skip 2ch-sp, 1dc, cc, turn.

Row 25: Ch1, 1dc, 1mtr, *1dc, 5mtr, 9dc, 5mtr; rep from * to last 3 sts, 1dc, 1mtr, 1dc, turn.

Row 26: As Row 2.

Row 27: Ch1, 1dc, ch2, skip 1 st, 2dc, ch6, skip 5 sts, 7dc, ch6, skip 5 sts, *3dc, ch6, skip 5 sts, 7dc, ch6, skip 5 sts; rep from * to last 4 sts, 2dc, ch2, skip 1 st, 1dc, turn.

Row 28: Ch1, 1dc, ch2, skip 2ch-sp, 2dc, ch6, skip 6ch-sp, 7dc, ch6, skip 6ch-sp, *3dc, ch6, skip 6ch-sp, 7dc, ch6, skip 6ch-sp; rep from * to last 4 sts, 2dc, ch2, skip 2ch-sp, 1dc, cc, turn.

Row 29: Ch1, 1dc, 1mtr, 2dc, 5mtr, 7dc, 5mtr, *3dc, 5mtr, 7dc, 5mtr; rep from * to last 4 sts, 2dc, 1mtr, 1dc, turn.

Row 30: As Row 2.

Row 31: Ch1, 1dc, ch2, skip 1 st, 3dc, ch6, skip 5 sts, *5dc, ch6, skip 5 sts; rep from * to last 5 sts, 3dc, ch2, skip 1 st, 1dc, turn.

Row 32: Ch1, 1dc, ch2, skip 2ch-sp, 3dc, ch6, skip 6ch-sp, *5dc, ch6, skip 6ch-sp; rep from * to last 5 sts, 3dc, ch2, skip 2ch-sp, 1dc, cc, turn.

Row 33: Ch1, 1dc, 1mtr, 3dc, 5mtr, *5dc, 5mtr; rep from * to last 5 sts, 3dc, 1mtr, 1dc, turn.

Row 34: As Row 2.

Row 35: Ch1, 1dc, ch2, skip 1 st, 4dc, ch6, skip 5 sts, 3dc, ch6, skip 5 sts, *7dc, ch6, skip 5 sts, 3dc, ch6, skip 5 sts; rep from * to last 6 sts, 4dc, ch2, skip 1 st, 1dc, turn.

Row 36: Ch1, 1dc, ch2, skip 2ch-sp, 4dc, ch6, skip 6ch-sp, 3dc, ch6, skip 6ch-sp, *7dc, ch6, skip 6ch-sp, 3dc, ch6, skip 6ch-sp; rep from * to last 6 sts, 4dc, ch2, skip 2ch-sp, 1dc, cc, turn.

Row 37: Ch1, 1dc, 1mtr, 4dc, 5mtr, 3dc, 5mtr, *7dc, 5mtr, 3dc, 5mtr; rep from * to last 6 sts, 4dc, 1mtr, 1dc, turn.

Row 38: As Row 2.

Row 39: Ch1, 1dc, ch2, skip 1 st, 5dc, ch6, skip 5 sts, 1dc, ch6, skip 5 sts, *9dc, ch6, skip 5 sts, 1dc, ch6, skip 5 sts; rep from * to last 7 sts, 5dc, ch2, skip 1 st, 1dc, turn.

Row 40: Ch1, 1dc, ch2, skip 2ch-sp, 5dc, ch6, skip 6ch-sp, 1dc, ch6, skip 6ch-sp, *9dc, ch6, skip 6ch-sp, 1dc, ch6, skip 6ch-sp; rep from * to last 7 sts, 5dc, ch2, skip 2ch-sp, 1dc, cc, turn.

Row 41: Ch1, 1dc, 1mtr, 5dc, 5mtr, 1dc, 5mtr, *9dc, 5mtr, 1dc, 5mtr; rep from * to last 7 sts, 5dc, 1mtr, 1dc, turn.

Row 42: As Row 2.

Row 43: Ch1, 1dc, ch7, skip 6 sts, 5dc, ch2, skip 1 st, 5dc, *ch10, skip 9 sts, 5dc, ch2, skip 1 st, 5dc; rep from * to last 7 sts, ch7, skip 6 sts, 1dc, turn.

Row 44: Ch1, 1dc, ch7, skip 7ch-sp, 5dc, ch2, skip 2ch-sp, 5dc, *ch10, skip 10ch-sp, 5dc, ch2, skip 2ch-sp, 5dc; rep from * to last 7 sts, ch7, skip 7ch-sp, 1dc, cc, turn.

Row 45: Ch1, 1dc, 6mtr, 5dc, 1mtr, 5dc, *9mtr, 5dc, 1mtr, 5dc; rep from * to last 7 sts, 6mtr, 1dc, turn.

Row 46: As Row 2.

Row 47: Ch1, 1dc, ch6, skip 5 sts, 5dc, ch4, skip 3 sts, 5dc, *ch8, skip 7 sts, 5dc, ch4, skip 3 sts, 5dc; rep from * to last 6 sts, ch6, skip 5 sts, 1dc, turn.

Row 48: Ch1, 1dc, ch6, skip 6ch-sp, 5dc, ch4, skip 4ch-sp, 5dc, *ch8, skip 8ch-sp, 5dc, ch4, skip 4ch-sp, 5dc; rep from * to last 6 sts, ch6, skip 6ch-sp, 1dc, cc, turn.

Row 49: Ch1, 1dc, 5mtr, 5dc, 3mtr, 5dc, *7mtr, 5dc, 3mtr, 5dc; rep from * to last 6 sts, 5mtr, 1dc, turn.

Row 50: As Row 2.

Row 51: Ch1, 1dc, ch5, skip 4 sts, 5dc, *ch6, skip 5 sts, 5dc; rep from * to last 5 sts, ch5, skip 4 sts, 1dc, turn.

Row 52: Ch1, 1dc, ch5, skip 5ch-sp, 5dc, *ch6, skip 6ch-sp, 5dc; rep from * to last 5 sts, ch5, skip 5ch-sp, 1dc, cc, turn.

Row 53: Ch1, 1dc, 4mtr, 5dc, *5mtr, 5dc; rep from * to last 5 sts, 4mtr, 1dc, turn.

Row 54: As Row 2.

Row 55: Ch1, 1dc, *ch4, skip 3 sts, 5dc, ch8, skip 7 sts, 5dc; rep from * to last 4 sts, ch4, skip 3 sts, 1dc, turn.

Row 56: Ch1, 1dc, *ch4, skip 4ch-sp, 5dc, ch8, skip 8ch-sp, 5dc; rep from * to last 4 sts, ch4, skip 4ch-sp, 1dc, cc, turn.

Row 57: Ch1, 1dc, *3mtr, 5dc, 7mtr, 5dc; rep from * to last 4 sts, 3mtr, 1dc, turn.

Row 58: As Row 2.

Row 59: Ch1, 1dc, ch3, skip 2 sts, 5dc, ch10, skip 9 sts, 5dc, *ch2, skip 1 st, 5dc, ch10, skip 9 sts, 5dc; rep from * to last 3 sts, ch3, skip 2 sts, 1dc, turn.

Row 60: Ch1, 1dc, ch3, skip 3ch-sp, 5dc, ch10, skip 10ch-sp, 5dc, *ch2, skip 2ch-sp, 5dc, ch10, skip 10ch-sp, 5dc; rep from * to last 3 sts, ch3, skip 3ch-sp, 1dc, cc, turn.

Row 61: Ch1, 1dc, 2mtr, 5dc, 9mtr, 5dc, *1mtr, 5dc, 9mtr, 5dc; rep from * to last 3 sts, 2mtr, 1dc, turn.

Row 62: As Row 2.

Row 63: Ch1, 1dc, ch2, skip 1 st, 5dc, ch6, skip 5 sts, 1dc, ch6, skip 5 sts, *9dc, ch6, skip 5 sts, 1dc, ch6, skip 5 sts; rep from * to last 7 sts, 5dc, ch2, skip 1 st, 1dc, turn.

Row 64: Ch1, 1dc, ch2, skip 2ch-sp, 5dc, ch6, skip 6ch-sp, 1dc, ch6, skip 6ch-sp, *9dc, ch6, skip 6ch-sp, 1dc, ch6, skip 6ch-sp; rep from * to last 7 sts, 5dc, ch2, skip 2ch-sp, 1dc, cc, turn.

Row 65: Ch1, 1dc, 1mtr, 5dc, 5mtr, 1dc, 5mtr, *9dc, 5mtr, 1dc, 5mtr; rep from * to last 7 sts, 5dc, 1mtr, 1dc, turn.

Row 66: As Row 2.

Row 67: Ch1, 1dc, ch2, skip 1 st, 4dc, ch6, skip 5 sts, 3dc, ch6, skip 5 sts, *7dc, ch6, skip 5 sts, 3dc, ch6, skip 5 sts; rep from * to last 6 sts, 4dc, ch2, skip 1 st, 1dc, turn.

Row 68: Ch1, 1dc, ch2, skip 2ch-sp, 4dc, ch6, skip 6ch-sp, 3dc, ch6, skip 6ch-sp, *7dc, ch6, skip 6ch-sp, 3dc, ch6, skip 6ch-sp; rep from * to last 6 sts, 4dc, ch2, skip 2ch-sp, 1dc, cc, turn.

Row 69: Ch1, 1dc, 1mtr, 4dc, 5mtr, 3dc, 5mtr, *7dc, 5mtr, 3dc, 5mtr; rep from * to last 6 sts, 4dc, 1mtr, 1dc, turn.

Row 70: As Row 2.

Row 71: Ch1, 1dc, ch2, skip 1 st, 3dc, ch6, skip 5 sts, *5dc, ch6, skip 5 sts; rep from * to last 5 sts, 3dc, ch2, skip 1 st, 1dc, turn.

Row 72: Ch1, 1dc, ch2, skip 2ch-sp, 3dc, ch6, skip 6ch-sp, *5dc, ch6, skip 6ch-sp; rep from * to last 5 sts, 3dc, ch2, skip 2ch-sp, 1dc, cc, turn.

Row 73: Ch1, 1dc, 1mtr, 3dc, 5mtr, *5dc, 5mtr; rep from * to last 5 sts, 3dc, 1mtr, 1dc, turn.

Row 74: As Row 2.

Row 75: Ch1, 1dc, ch2, skip 1 st, 2dc, ch6, skip 5 sts, 7dc, ch6, skip 5 sts, *3dc, ch6, skip 5 sts, 7dc, ch6, skip 5 sts; rep from * to last 4 sts, 2dc, ch2, skip 1 st, 1dc, turn.

Row 76: Ch1, 1dc, ch2, skip 2ch-sp, 2dc, ch6, skip 6ch-sp, 7dc, ch6, skip 6ch-sp, *3dc, ch6, skip 6ch-sp, 7dc, ch6, skip 6ch-sp; rep from * to last 4 sts, 2dc, ch2, skip 2ch-sp, 1dc, cc, turn.

Row 77: Ch1, 1dc, 1mtr, 2dc, 5mtr, 7dc, 5mtr, *3dc, 5mtr, 7dc, 5mtr; rep from * to last 4 sts, 2dc, 1mtr, 1dc, turn.

Row 78: As Row 2.

Row 79: Ch1, 1dc, ch2, skip 1 st, *1dc, ch6, skip 5 sts, 9dc, ch6, skip 5 sts; rep from * to last 3 sts, 1dc, ch2, skip 1 st, 1dc, turn.

Row 80: Ch1, 1dc, ch2, skip 2ch-sp, *1dc, ch6, skip 6ch-sp, 9dc, ch6, skip 6ch-sp; rep from * to last 3 sts, 1dc, ch2, skip 2ch-sp, 1dc, cc, turn.

Row 81: Ch1, 1dc, 1mtr, *1dc, 5mtr, 9dc, 5mtr; rep from * to last 3 sts, 1dc, 1mtr, 1dc, turn.

Row 82: As Row 2.

Rows 83 to 242: Rep Rows 3 to 82 twice more.

Fasten off yarns and weave in ends.

EDGING

Round 1 (RS): Join B with a slst in top right hand st on edge of throw, ch1 (does not count as st throughout), (1dc, ch2, 1dc) in same st, 1dc in each st to last st on top edge, (1dc, ch2, 1dc) in last st, rotate work 90 degrees, 1dc in each of next three row ends, *skip next row end, 1dc in each of next four row ends; rep from * to end of long side, finishing on any st in rep, rotate work, (1dc, ch2, 1dc) in first st on bottom edge, 1dc in each st to last st on bottom edge, (1dc, ch2, 1dc) in last st, rotate work, 1dc in each of next three row ends, **skip next row end, 1dc in each of next four row ends; rep from ** to end of long side, finishing on any st in rep, slst to beg dc, turn.

Round 2 (WS): Ch1, *1dc in each st to 2ch-sp, (1dc, ch2, 1dc) in ch-sp; rep from * around to end, slst to beg dc.

Fasten off and weave in ends.

POMPOMS

(make 4)

Using A and pompom maker, make four pompoms. Trim to shape, and sew one to each corner of the Throw.

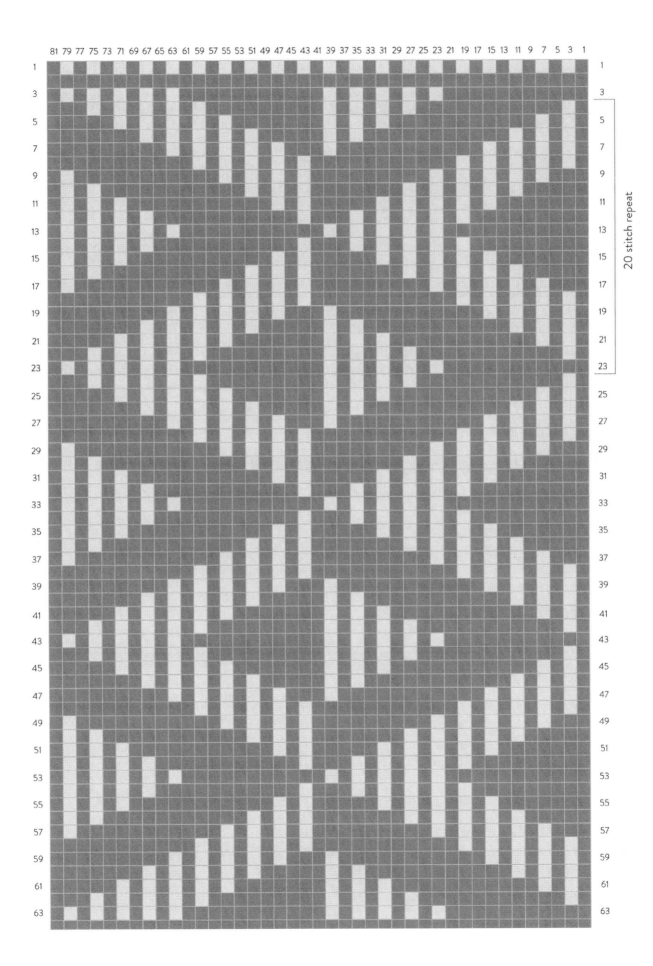

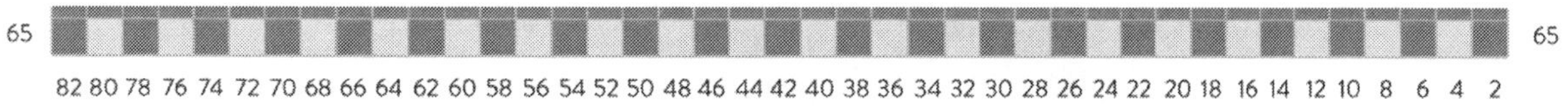

65   65

82 80 78 76 74 72 70 68 66 64 62 60 58 56 54 52 50 48 46 44 42 40 38 36 34 32 30 28 26 24 22 20 18 16 14 12 10 8 6 4 2

KEY

A

B

Each square represents a stitch.

To work from this chart, rotate it 90 degrees clockwise. Read all odd-numbered (RS) rows from right to left, and all even-numbered (WS) rows from left to right.

Work rows 1 to 82 to start, and on subsequent repeats work rows 3 to 82.

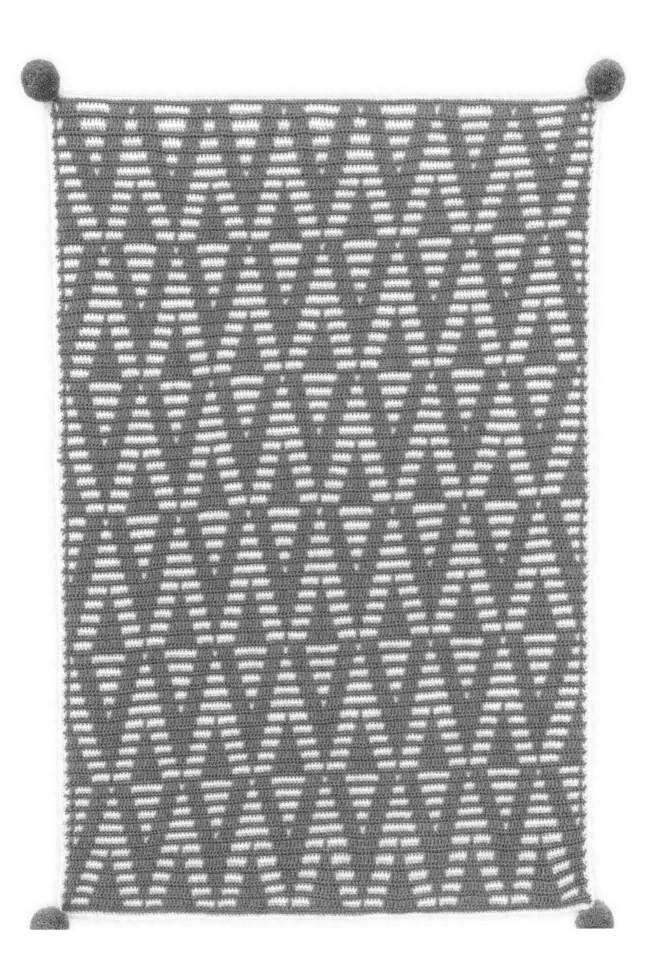

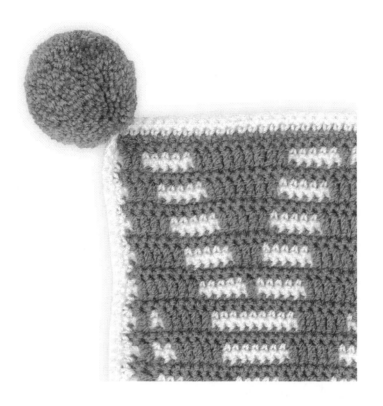

TOP TIP

This would be perfect for a first mosaic crochet project!

Try a new colourway

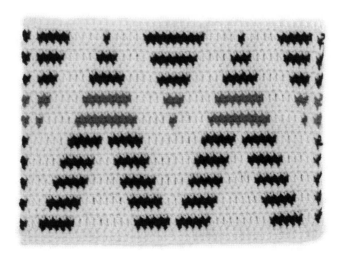

CHEEKY MONOCHROME

All geometric designs seem to look amazing in black and white. It's a timeless combination, effortlessly cool. To take monochrome to a new level add a pop of bright pink, just for a few rows, to create a bit of cheeky fabulousness.

SPIN-OFF PROJECT:
Handy Little Clutch

SKILL LEVEL:

Such a useful little bag – mine goes everywhere with me. Money, keys, phone, lippy, all the essentials fit in perfectly. I've added a wristlet strap to make this super-portable, and a pompom just for a bit of fancy nonsense. This is a great design to customize to your own style. You could even line your clutch with waterproof fabric to make it the most stylish travel wash bag on the road.

YOU WILL NEED

YARN

Scheepjes Catona (100% cotton), 4-ply/sport, 50g (125m/136yds), in the following shade:

Spruce (244); 2 balls (A)

Scheepjes Stone Washed (78% cotton/22% acrylic), 4-ply/sport, 50g (130m/142yds), in the following shade:

Moon Stone (801); 1 ball (B)

Scheepjes River Washed (78% cotton/22% acrylic), 4-ply/sport, 50g (130m/142yds), in the following shade:

Yarra (949); 1 ball (C)

HOOK

3mm crochet hook

OTHER TOOLS AND MATERIALS

Approx. 45 x 35cm (17¾ x 13¾in) of lining (or waterproof) fabric

Sewing needle, thread and pins

Sewing machine (optional)

30cm (12in) dark blue zip

Purple wristlet strap (optional)

35mm (1⅜in) pompom maker

PATTERN MULTIPLES

Pattern works to a multiple of 20 stitches + 6 stitches for the starting chain.

TENSION (GAUGE)

19 sts and 23 rows measure 10 x 10cm (4 x 4in) over patt using a 3mm hook.

FINISHED SIZE

Each panel measures 21 x 32cm (8¼ x 12½in) before assembly

Bag measures approx. 19 x 30cm (7½ x 12in)

Note

First, two crocheted panels are worked for the front and back of the bag, then a lining is made with a zip and inserted. A hanging loop and decorative pompom are added to finish.

There's quite a lot of sewing with this project – but you don't have to line the bag and/or insert the zip, you can just add a couple of buttons or magnetic fasteners to the top if you prefer. For a little fold-over top instead, add a few more rows of double crochet in C along the top edges. It's up to you how you customize your own handy little clutch!

INSTRUCTIONS
Panel

(make 2)

Using A, ch66.

Row 1 (RS): 1dc in second ch from hook and in each ch to end, turn. (65 sts)

Rows 2 to 5: Ch1 (does not count as st throughout), 1dc in each st to end, turn.

Now follow Misty Mountains Throw patt, starting at Row 2 (using A) and finishing at end of Row 42, using A and B as indicated.

Fasten off B, do not fasten off A.

Next 2 rows: Using A, ch1, 1dc in each st to end, turn. Cc to C at end of these 2 rows.

Fasten off A.

Next 2 rows: Using C, ch1, 1dc in each st to end, turn.

Fasten off and weave in all ends.

ASSEMBLY
To ensure the lining is the correct size, measure the height and width of one crocheted panel and cut two pieces of lining fabric to the same width as the panel, but add 1cm (⅜in) to the height for the zip insert.

Panels

Place the two crocheted panels RS together. Using a needle and thread, pin or tack (baste) along the side, bottom, and other side to hold them together. Either hand or machine sew around these three sides with a 1cm (⅜in) seam allowance.

To add depth to the bag (if required), make box corners as follows: With WS still facing out, flatten each bottom corner into a triangle, so the side seam is directly on top of the bottom seam. With the seams opened out to reduce bulk, sew a small straight line across the triangle 1cm (⅜in) down from the tip. Sew the loose corners to the bottom edge to hold them in place.

Turn the bag RS out.

Lining

Lay one piece of fabric on a flat surface with RS facing up and with the long edges at top and bottom. Align one edge of the zip with the top edge of the fabric, also with RS facing up. Pin or tack, then sew the zip to the fabric along this top edge. Repeat with the other piece of fabric and the other edge of the zip.

Hold the two pieces of fabric with RS together so that they are exactly lined up, one on top of the other. Pin or tack around all four edges to hold everything in place, then place the lining inside the bag to gauge what seam allowance is needed to ensure the lining fits properly. Remove the lining and sew from just under the zip down the side, along the bottom and up other side edge to just under the zip. Remove the tacking and press all seams open. Make box corners as before if necessary.

Insert the lining into the bag and sew the zip securely to the top edge of the bag with small running stitches, leaving a 7.5cm (3in) gap at one end.

Hanging loop for wristlet strap

Using C, ch3, 1dc in second ch from hook, 1dc in third ch from hook, turn. (2 sts)

Next 6 rows: Ch1 (does not count as st), 1dc in each dc, turn.

Fasten off and weave in ends.

Fold the strip in half and insert the ends into the gap at the end of the bag, between the bag and the lining, so a loop is visible on the outside. Sew up the final gap with the hanging loop in place. Attach wristlet strap through hanging loop.

Pompom

Using C, make a small pompom.

Using A, ch30, leaving long tails for sewing.

Fasten off.

Insert one tail through the zip end, pull the ch halfway through, then thread both tails onto a needle and sew through the centre of the pompom to secure so that the chains touch the pompom. Knot securely and fasten off the ends.

TOP TIP

A great stash-busting project! Any cotton yarn works really well for this clutch.

Floating Points Throw

I think it's fairly obvious that my love for crocheting huge throws is limitless, but there are definite 'lulls' in energy levels: 20 hours into a 30 hour make, it can get a bit, dare I say, samey? This is where my preferred pick-me-up of dance music comes in. I was always a bit of a raver back in the mists of time (the 1990s) and now at a more 'mature' age I still turn it up too loud and kitchen-dance, much to the chagrin of the Other Half. Still, we have both learned to tolerate each other's music taste (I'll say that for the sake of harmonious living). This throw is inspired by the amazing musician Sam Shepherd aka Floating Points.

YOU WILL NEED

YARN

Scheepjes Colour Crafter (100% acrylic), DK/light worsted, 100g (300m/328yds), in the following shades:

Pollare (2018); 4 balls (A)

Sint Niklaas (2019); 3 balls (B)

Eelde (1422); 2 balls (C)

HOOK

5.5mm crochet hook

OTHER TOOLS

45mm (1¾in) pompom maker

PATTERN MULTIPLES

Pattern works to a multiple of 16 stitches + 2 stitches for the starting chain.

TENSION (GAUGE)

14 sts and 18 rows measure 10 x 10cm (4 x 4in) over patt using a 5.5mm hook.

FINISHED SIZE

Approx. 106 x 136cm (41½ x 53½in)

Note

Yarns A and B are used to make the main throw, then it is edged in C. The 20 pompoms are made in C and attached to the short ends of the throw to finish.

INSTRUCTIONS

Using A, ch146.

Row 1 (RS): 1dc in second ch from hook and in each ch to end, turn. (145 sts)

Row 2 (WS): Ch1 (does not count as st throughout), 1dc in each st to end, cc to B, turn.

Row 3: Ch1, 1dc, ch2, skip 1 st, 2dc, ch10, skip 9 sts, *7dc, ch10, skip 9 sts; rep from * to last 4 sts, 2dc, ch2, skip 1 st, 1dc, turn.

Row 4: Ch1, 1dc, ch2, skip 2ch-sp, 2dc, ch10, skip 10ch-sp, *7dc, ch10, skip 10ch-sp; rep from * to last 4 sts, 2dc, ch2, skip 2ch-sp, 1dc, cc to A, turn.

Row 5: Ch1, 1dc, 1mtr, 2dc, 9mtr, *7dc, 9mtr; rep from * to last 4 sts, 2dc, 1mtr, 1dc, turn.

Row 6: As Row 2.

Row 7: Ch1, 1dc, ch2, skip 1 st, 4dc, ch6, skip 5 sts, *11dc, ch6, skip 5 sts; rep from * to last 6 sts, 4dc, ch2, skip 1 st, 1dc, turn.

Row 8: Ch1, 1dc, ch2, skip 2ch-sp, 4dc, ch6, skip 6ch-sp, *11dc, ch6, skip 6ch-sp; rep from * to last 6 sts, 4dc, ch2, skip 2ch-sp, 1dc, cc, turn.

Row 9: Ch1, 1dc, 1mtr, 4dc, 5mtr, *11dc, 5mtr; rep from * to last 6 sts, 4dc, 1mtr, 1dc, turn.

Row 10: As Row 2.

Row 11: Ch1, 1dc, ch2, skip 1 st, 5dc, ch4, skip 3 sts, *13dc, ch4, skip 3 sts; rep from * to last 7 sts, 5dc, ch2, skip 1 st, 1dc, turn.

Row 12: Ch1, 1dc, ch2, skip 2ch-sp, 5dc, ch4, skip 4ch-sp, *13dc, ch4, skip 4ch-sp; rep from * to last 7 sts, 5dc, ch2, skip 2ch-sp, 1dc, cc, turn.

Row 13: Ch1, 1dc, 1mtr, 5dc, 3mtr, *13dc, 3mtr; rep from * to last 7 sts, 5dc, 1mtr, 1dc, turn.

Row 14: As Row 2.

Row 15: Ch1, 1dc, ch2, skip 1 st, 5dc, ch4, skip 3 sts, *13dc, ch4, skip 3 sts; rep from * to last 7 sts, 5dc, ch2, skip 1 st, 1dc, turn.

Row 16: Ch1, 1dc, ch2, skip 2ch-sp, 5dc, ch4, skip 4ch-sp, *13dc, ch4, skip 4ch-sp; rep from * to last 7 sts, 5dc, ch2, skip 2ch-sp, 1dc, cc, turn.

Row 17: Ch1, 1dc, 1mtr, 5dc, 3mtr, *13dc, 3mtr; rep from * to last 7 sts, 5dc, 1mtr, 1dc, turn.

Row 18: As Row 2.

Row 19: Ch1, 1dc, ch2, skip 1 st, 4dc, ch6, skip 5 sts, *11dc, ch6, skip 5 sts; rep from * to last 6 sts, 4dc, ch2, skip 1 st, 1dc, turn.

Row 20: Ch1, 1dc, ch2, skip 2ch-sp, 4dc, ch6, skip 6ch-sp, *11dc, ch6, skip 6ch-sp; rep from * to last 6 sts, 4dc, ch2, skip 2ch-sp, 1dc, cc, turn.

Row 21: Ch1, 1dc, 1mtr, 4dc, 5mtr, *11dc, 5mtr; rep from * to last 6 sts, 4dc, 1mtr, 1dc, turn.

Row 22: As Row 2.

Row 23: Ch1, 1dc, ch2, skip 1 st, 2dc, ch10, skip 9 sts, *7dc, ch10, skip 9 sts; rep from * to last 4 sts, 2dc, ch2, skip 1 st, 1dc, turn.

Row 24: Ch1, 1dc, ch2, skip 2ch-sp, 2dc, ch10, skip 10ch-sp, *7dc, ch10, skip 10ch-sp; rep from * to last 4 sts, 2dc, ch2, skip 2ch-sp, 1dc, cc, turn.

Row 25: Ch1, 1dc, 1mtr, 2dc, 9mtr, *7dc, 9mtr; rep from * to last 4 sts, 2dc, 1mtr, 1dc, turn.

Row 26: As Row 2.

Row 27: Ch1, 1dc, ch5, skip 4 sts, 7dc, *ch10, skip 9 sts, 7dc; rep from * to last 5 sts, ch5, skip 4 sts, 1dc, turn.

Row 28: Ch1, 1dc, ch5, skip 5ch-sp, 7dc, *ch10, skip 10ch-sp, 7dc; rep from * to last 5 sts, ch5, skip 5ch-sp, 1dc, cc, turn.

Row 29: Ch1, 1dc, 4mtr, 7dc, *9mtr, 7dc; rep from * to last 5 sts, 4mtr, 1dc, turn.

Row 30: As Row 2.

Row 31: Ch1, 1dc, ch3, skip 2 sts, 11dc, *ch6, skip 5 sts, 11dc; rep from * to last 3 sts, ch3, skip 2 sts, 1dc, turn.

Row 32: Ch1, 1dc, ch3, skip 3ch-sp, 11dc, *ch6, skip 6ch-sp, 11dc; rep from * to last 3 sts, ch3, skip 3ch-sp, 1dc, cc, turn.

Row 33: Ch1, 1dc, 2mtr, 11dc, *5mtr, 11dc; rep from * to last 3 sts, 2mtr, 1dc, turn.

Row 34: As Row 2.

Row 35: Ch1, 1dc, ch2, skip 1 st, 13dc, *ch4, skip 3 sts, 13dc; rep from * to last 2 sts, ch2, skip 1 st, 1dc, turn.

Row 36: Ch1, 1dc, ch2, skip 2ch-sp, 13dc, *ch4, skip 4ch-sp, 13dc; rep from * to last 2 sts, ch2, skip 2ch-sp, 1dc, cc, turn.

Row 37: Ch1, 1dc, 1mtr, 13dc, *3mtr, 13dc; rep from * to last 2 sts, 1mtr, 1dc, turn.

Row 38: As Row 2.

Row 39: Ch1, 1dc, ch2, skip 1 st, 13dc, *ch4, skip 3 sts, 13dc; rep from * to last 2 sts, ch2, skip 1 st, 1dc, turn.

Row 40: Ch1, 1dc, ch2, skip 2ch-sp, 13dc, *ch4, skip 4ch-sp, 13dc; rep from * to last 2 sts, ch2, skip 2ch-sp, 1dc, cc, turn.

Row 41: Ch1, 1dc, 1mtr, 13dc, *3mtr, 13dc; rep from * to last 2 sts, 1mtr, 1dc, turn.

Row 42: As Row 2.

Row 43: Ch1, 1dc, ch3, skip 2 sts, 11dc, *ch6, skip 5 sts, 11dc; rep from * to last 3 sts, ch3, skip 2 sts, 1dc, turn.

Row 44: Ch1, 1dc, ch3, skip 3ch-sp, 11dc, *ch6, skip 6ch-sp, 11dc; rep from * to last 3 sts, ch3, skip 3ch-sp, 1dc, cc, turn.

Row 45: Ch1, 1dc, 2mtr, 11dc, *5mtr, 11dc; rep from * to last 3 sts, 2mtr, 1dc, turn.

Row 46: As Row 2.

Row 47: Ch1, 1dc, ch5, skip 4 sts, 7dc, *ch10, skip 9 sts, 7dc; rep from * to last 5 sts, ch5, skip 4 sts, 1dc, turn.

Row 48: Ch1, 1dc, ch5, skip 5ch-sp, 7dc, *ch10, skip 10ch-sp, 7dc; rep from * to last 5 sts, ch5, skip 5ch-sp, 1dc, cc, turn.

Row 49: Ch1, 1dc, 4mtr, 7dc, *9mtr, 7dc; rep from * to last 5 sts, 4mtr, 1dc, turn.

Row 50: As Row 2.

Rows 51 to 242: Rep Rows 3 to 50 four more times.

Fasten off A and B.

EDGING

Round 1 (RS): Join C with a slst in top right hand st on edge of throw, ch1 (does not count as st throughout), (1dc, ch2, 1dc) in same st, 1dc in each st to last st on top edge, (1dc, ch2, 1dc) in last st, rotate work 90 degrees, 1dc in each of next three row ends, *skip next row end, 1dc in each of next four row ends; rep from * to end of long side, finishing on any st in rep, rotate work, (1dc, ch2, 1dc) in first st on bottom edge, 1dc in each st to last st on bottom edge, (1dc, ch2, 1dc) in last st, rotate work, 1dc in each of next three row ends, **skip next row end, 1dc in each of next four row ends; rep from ** to end of long side, finishing on any st in rep, slst to beg dc, turn.

Round 2 (WS): Ch1, *1dc in each st to 2ch-sp, (1dc, ch2, 1dc) in ch-sp; rep from * around to end, slst to beg dc.

Fasten off and weave in ends.

POMPOMS

(make 20)

Using C and the pompom maker, make 20 pompoms. Trim to shape, and then sew 10 along each short side of the throw at regular intervals.

Fasten off and weave in all ends.

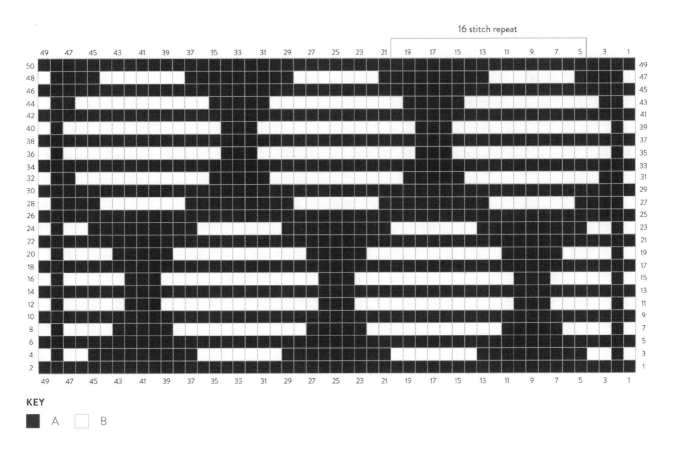

KEY

■ A ☐ B

Each square represents a stitch.

Read all odd-numbered (RS) rows from right to left, and all even-numbered (WS) rows from left to right.

Work rows 1 to 50 to start, and on subsequent repeats work rows 3 to 50.

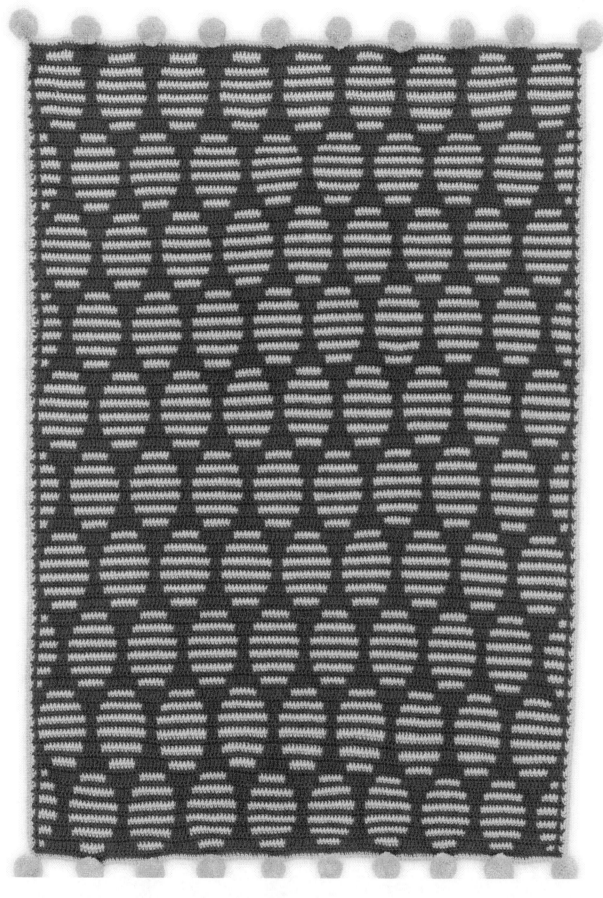

TOP TIP

This is a simple pattern that is still very effective and would be a great introduction to mosaic crochet.

TOP TIP

Using a gradient yarn as your background colour on this pattern could create a fantastic outer space effect!

Try a new colourway

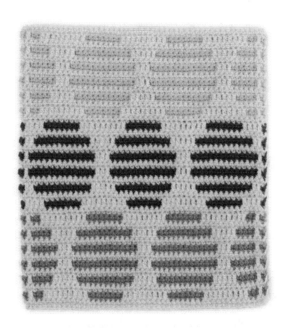

EXPLORING ONE COLOUR

Immersing yourself in one particular colour can produce beautiful effects. Here different shades of green, from soft mint right through to forest green, all work together to create a calm yet intriguing palette.

SPIN-OFF PROJECT:
Yayoi Scarf

SKILL LEVEL:

This cute little scarf is inspired by Japanese contemporary artist Yayoi Kusama, sometimes referred to as 'the princess of polka dots'. I saw a stunning exhibition of her work at Tate Modern in London a few years ago. From rooms full of mirrors to painted pumpkins, infinity nets and soft sculptures, there's a wonderful weirdness and freshness to her work. And a LOT of polka dots.

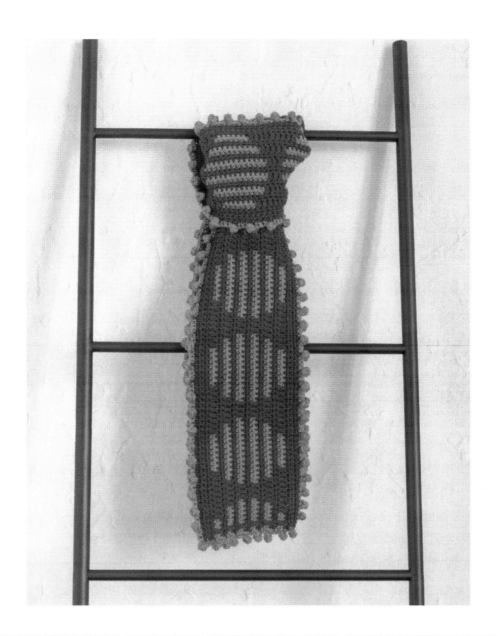

YOU WILL NEED

YARN

Scheepjes Merino Soft (50% superwash merino wool/25% microfibre/25% acrylic), DK/light worsted, 50g (105m/114yds), in the following shades:

Carney (636); 2 balls (A)

van Eyck (645); 2 balls (B)

HOOK

4mm crochet hook

5mm crochet hook

OTHER TOOLS

Stitch markers

PATTERN MULTIPLES
Pattern works to a multiple of 16 stitches + 2 stitches for the starting chain.

TENSION (GAUGE)
14 sts and 24 rows measure 10 x 10cm (4 x 4in) over patt using a 5mm hook.

FINISHED SIZE
Approx. 14 x 150cm (5½ x 59in) after blocking

Notes
If you want to make a longer scarf, calculate your starting chain using the Pattern Multiples; you will need more of both A and B (this version used almost all of A). As you are starting with a very long chain, it's advisable to place a stitch marker in every 50th chain so you don't lose count.

Once the scarf is made, it is edged with a bobble edging, then blocked to size if desired.

SPECIAL ABBREVIATION
MB, make bobble: Ch3, [yarn round hook, insert hook in third chain from hook, yarn round hook, pull up a loop] 3 times, yarn round hook, draw hook through all loops on hook, chain 1, slip stitch in third chain from hook to close bobble

INSTRUCTIONS
Using A and 5mm hook, ch210.

Row 1 (RS): 1dc in second ch from hook and in each ch to end, turn. (209 sts)

Rows 2 and 3: Ch1 (does not count as st throughout), 1dc in each st to end, turn.

Now follow Floating Points Throw patt, starting at Row 2 (using A) and finishing at end of Row 26, using A and B as indicated. Do not cc to B at end of Row 26, keep A on hook.

Next 2 rows: Using A, ch1, 1dc in each st to end, turn.

Fasten off and weave in all ends.

EDGING
Using 4mm hook and with WS facing throughout, join B with a slst to any st on edge.

Ch1, *1dc in each of next 3 sts, MB; rep from * around edge, slst to beg dc. Fasten off and weave in ends, block to measurements if desired.

TOP TIP

This pattern is easy to adapt, so make this scarf longer or shorter to suit your style.

Sun Spot Throw

SKILL LEVEL:

Colour clash! Deep red against punchy neon pink! I absolutely love this colour combination – this is a design as much about the dark negative spaces created as it is about the bright, burning sun spots. Of course, it would work well in more subtle, sophisticated colours but, as its name suggests, this is one bright star that loves to shine. It's one of the trickier throws in this book as the pattern runs vertically. Saying that though, I think it's definitely worth the extra concentration as the end result is rather amazing; dazzling even.

161

YOU WILL NEED

YARN

Scheepjes Colour Crafter (100% Acrylic), DK/light worsted, 100g (300m/328yd), in the following shades:

Kampen (1035); 3 balls (A)

Hilversum (1257); 4 balls (B)

HOOK

5.5mm hook

OTHER TOOLS

65mm (2½in) pompom maker

PATTERN MULTIPLES

Pattern works to a multiple of 20 stitches + 2 stitches for the starting chain.

TENSION (GAUGE)

14 sts and 18 rows measure 10 x 10cm (4 x 4in) over patt using a 5.5mm hook.

FINISHED SIZE

Approx. 102 x 134cm (40¼ x 52¾in)

Note

Yarns A and B work together in this intricate pattern. Keep a close eye on your stitch counts in the first few rows because there are many single stitches and short chains to make. Once the main throw is made, it is finished with a simple edging in B and a pompom is added on each corner.

INSTRUCTIONS

Using A, ch142.

Row 1 (RS): 1dc in second ch from hook and in each ch to end, turn. (141 sts)

Row 2 (WS): Ch1 (does not count as st throughout), 1dc in each st to end, cc to B, turn.

Row 3: Ch1, 1dc, ch6, skip 5 sts, 1dc, [ch2, skip 1 st, 1dc] 4 times, *ch12, skip 11 sts, 1dc, [ch2, skip 1 st, 1dc] 4 times; rep from * to last 6 sts, ch6, skip 5 sts, 1dc, turn.

Row 4: Ch1, 1dc, ch6, skip 6ch-sp, 1dc, [ch2, skip 2ch-sp, 1dc] 4 times, *ch12, skip 12ch-sp, 1dc, [ch2, skip 2ch-sp, 1dc] 4 times; rep from * to last 6 sts, ch6, skip 6ch-sp, 1dc, cc to A, turn.

Row 5: Ch1, 1dc, 5mtr, ch2, skip 1 st, [1mtr, ch2, skip 1 st] 4 times, *11mtr, ch2, skip 1 st, [1mtr, ch2, skip 1 st] 4 times; rep from * to last 6 sts, 5mtr, 1dc, turn.

Row 6: Ch1, 6dc, ch2, skip 2ch-sp, [1dc, ch2, skip 2ch-sp] 4 times, *11dc, ch2, skip 2ch-sp, [1dc, ch2, skip 2ch-sp] 4 times; rep from * to last 6 sts, 6dc, cc, turn.

Row 7: Ch1, 1dc, ch4, skip 3 sts, 1dc, [ch2, skip 1 st, 1mtr] 5 times, ch2, skip 1 st, 1dc, *ch8, skip 7 sts, 1dc, [ch2, skip 1 st, 1mtr] 5 times, ch2, skip 1 st, 1dc; rep from * to last 4 sts, ch4, skip 3 sts, 1dc, turn.

Row 8: Ch1, 1dc, ch4, skip 4ch-sp, 1dc, [ch2, skip 2ch-sp, 1dc] 6 times, *ch8, skip 8ch-sp, 1dc, [ch2, skip 2ch-sp, 1dc] 6 times; rep from * to last 4 sts, ch4, skip 4ch-sp, 1dc, cc, turn.

Row 9: Ch1, 1dc, 3mtr, ch2, skip 1 st, [1mtr, ch2, skip 1 st] 6 times, *7mtr, ch2, skip 1 st, [1mtr, ch2, skip 1 st] 6 times; rep from * to last 4 sts, 3mtr, 1dc, turn.

Row 10: Ch1, 4dc, ch2, skip 2ch-sp, [1dc, ch2, skip 2ch-sp] 6 times, *7dc, ch2, skip 2ch-sp, [1dc, ch2, skip 2ch-sp] 6 times; rep from * to last 4 sts, 4dc, cc, turn.

Row 11: Ch1, 1dc, ch2, skip 1 st, 1dc, [ch2, skip 1 st, 1mtr] 7 times, ch2, skip 1 st, 1dc, *ch4, skip 3 sts, 1dc, [ch2, skip 1 st, 1mtr] 7 times, ch2, skip 1 st, 1dc; rep from * to last 2 sts, ch2, skip 1 st, 1dc, turn.

Row 12: Ch1, 1dc, [ch2, skip 2ch-sp, 1dc] 9 times, *ch4, skip 4ch-sp, 1dc, [ch2, skip 2ch-sp, 1dc] 8 times; rep from * to last 2 sts, ch2, skip 2ch-sp, 1dc, cc, turn.

Row 13: Ch1, 1dc, [1mtr, ch2, skip 1 st] 9 times, *3mtr, ch2, skip 1 st, [1mtr, ch2, skip 1 st] 8 times; rep from * to last 2 sts, 1mtr, 1dc, turn.

Row 14: Ch1, 2dc, ch2, skip 2ch-sp, [1dc, ch2, skip 2ch-sp] 8 times, *3dc, ch2, skip 2ch-sp, [1dc, ch2, skip 2ch-sp] 8 times; rep from * to last 2 sts, 2dc, cc, turn.

Row 15: Ch1, 1dc, [ch2, skip 1 st, 1mtr] 9 times, *ch4, skip 3 sts, 1mtr, [ch2, skip 1 st, 1mtr] 8 times; rep from * to last 2 sts, ch2, skip 1 st, 1dc, turn.

Row 16: Ch1, 1dc, [ch2, skip 2ch-sp, 1dc] 9 times, *ch4, skip 4ch-sp, 1dc, [ch2, skip 2ch-sp, 1dc] 8 times; rep from * to last 2 sts, ch2, skip 2ch-sp, 1dc, cc, turn.

Rows 17 to 24: Rep Rows 13 to 16 twice more.

Row 25: Ch1, [1dc, 1mtr] twice, [ch2, skip 1 st, 1mtr] 7 times, 1dc, *3mtr, 1dc, 1mtr, [ch2, skip 1 st, 1mtr] 7 times, 1dc; rep from * to last 2 sts, 1mtr, 1dc, turn.

Row 26: Ch1, 4dc, ch2, skip 2ch-sp, [1dc, ch2, skip 2ch-sp] 6 times, *7dc, ch2, skip 2ch-sp, [1dc, ch2, skip 2ch-sp] 6 times; rep from * to last 4 sts, 4dc, cc, turn.

Row 27: Ch1, 1dc, ch4, skip 3 sts, 1mtr, [ch2, skip 1 st, 1mtr] 6 times, *ch8, skip 7 sts, 1mtr, [ch2, skip 1 st, 1mtr] 6 times; rep from * to last 4 sts, ch4, skip 3 sts, 1dc, turn.

Row 28: Ch1, 1dc, ch4, skip 4ch-sp, 1dc, [ch2, skip 2ch-sp, 1dc] 6 times, *ch8, skip 8ch-sp, 1dc, [ch2, skip 2ch-sp, 1dc] 6 times; rep from * to last 4 sts, ch4, skip 4ch-sp, 1dc, cc, turn.

Row 29: Ch1, 1dc, 3mtr, 1dc, 1mtr, [ch2, skip 1 st, 1mtr] 5 times, 1dc, *7mtr, 1dc, 1mtr, [ch2, skip 1 st, 1mtr] 5 times, 1dc; rep from * to last 4 sts, 3mtr, 1dc, turn.

Row 30: Ch1, 6dc, ch2, skip 2ch-sp, [1dc, ch2, skip 2ch-sp] 4 times, *11dc, ch2, skip 2ch-sp, [1dc, ch2, skip 2ch-sp] 4 times; rep from * to last 6 sts, 6dc, cc, turn.

Row 31: Ch1, 1dc, ch6, skip 5 sts, 1mtr, [ch2, skip 1 st, 1mtr] 4 times, *ch12, skip 11 sts, 1mtr, [ch2, skip 1 st, 1mtr] 4 times; rep from * to last 6 sts, ch6, skip 5 sts, 1dc, turn.

Row 32: Ch1, 1dc, ch6, skip 6ch-sp, 1dc, [ch2, skip 2ch-sp, 1dc] 4 times, *ch12, skip 12ch-sp, 1dc, [ch2, skip 2ch-sp, 1dc] 4 times; rep from * to last 6 sts, ch6, skip 6ch-sp, 1dc, cc, turn. Fasten off B.

Row 33: Ch1, 1dc, 5mtr, 1dc, [1mtr, 1dc] 4 times, *11mtr, 1dc, [1mtr, 1dc] 4 times; rep from * to last 6 sts, 5mtr, 1dc, turn.

Rows 34 to 36: Using A, ch1, 1dc in each st to end, turn. Cc to B at end of Row 36.

Rows 37 to 238: Rep Rows 3 to 36 a further 5 times, then rep Rows 3 to 34 once more.

Fasten off both yarns and weave in all ends.

EDGING

Round 1 (RS): Join B with a slst in top right hand st on edge of throw, ch1 (does not count as st throughout), (1dc, ch2, 1dc) in same st, 1dc in each st to last st on top edge, (1dc, ch2, 1dc) in last st, rotate work 90 degrees, 1dc in each of next three row ends, *skip next row end, 1dc in each of next four row ends; rep from * to end of long side, finishing on any st in rep, rotate work, (1dc, ch2, 1dc) in first st on bottom edge, 1dc in each st to last st on bottom edge, (1dc, ch2, 1dc) in last st, rotate work, 1dc in each of next three row ends, **skip next row end, 1dc in each of next four row ends; rep from ** to end of long side, finishing on any st in rep, slst to beg dc, turn.

Round 2 (WS): Ch1, *1dc in each st to 2ch-sp, (1dc, ch2, 1dc) in ch-sp; rep from * around to end, slst to beg dc.

Fasten off and weave in all ends.

POMPOMS
(make 4)

Using B and pompom maker, make four pompoms. Trim to shape, and sew one to each corner of the throw.

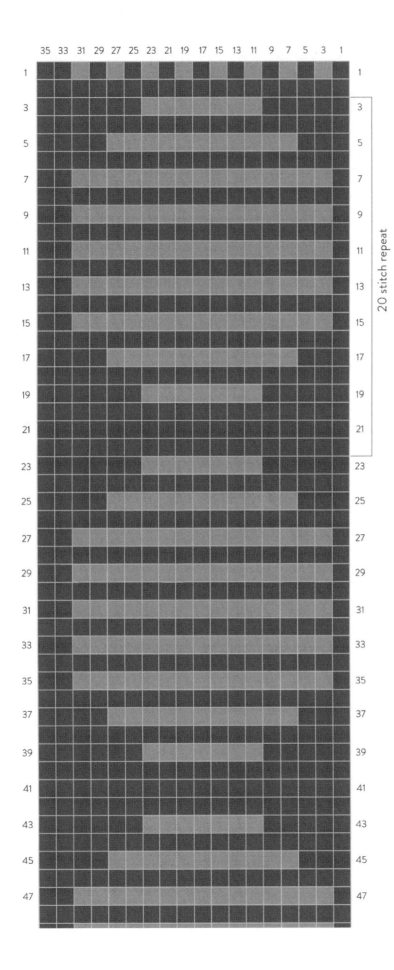

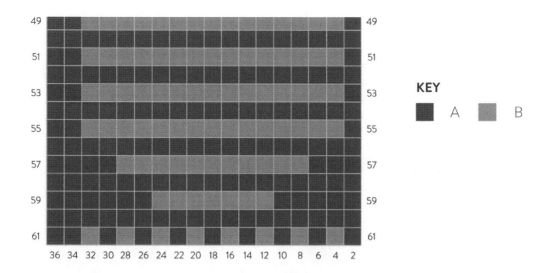

Each square represents a stitch.

To work from this chart, rotate it by 90 degrees clockwise. Read all odd-numbered (RS) rows from right to left, and all even-numbered (WS) rows from left to right.

Work rows 1 to 36 to start, and on subsequent repeats work rows 3 to 36.

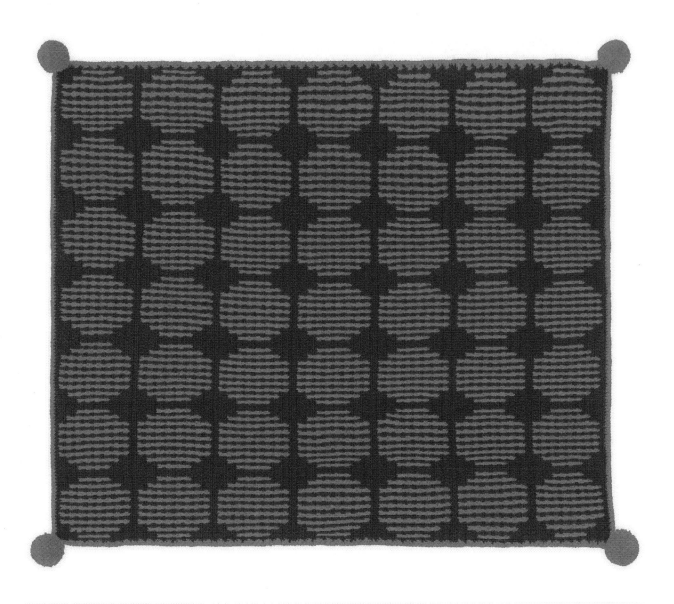

TOP TIP

A more challenging pattern – take your time with the counting on this one.

Try a new colourway

GO RETRO!

Pushing your colour boundaries can lead to new combinations that you might just fall in love with. Brown has never really been on my favourite colour list, but it looks great here in this 1970s retro revival palette combined with duck egg blue and gold.

SPIN-OFF PROJECT:
Fancy Footstool

SKILL LEVEL:

I couldn't write this book without giving my lazy, grumpy cat, Hank Deluxe, a mention. For those of you who haven't had the pleasure of meeting him, let's just say that, like most cats, he's a professional lounger who likes to make himself comfortable on whatever work is most important. Annoying, maybe. Gorgeous, definitely. So this footstool is for you, Hank Deluxe. May you always be comfortable and pampered and loved.

YOU WILL NEED

YARN

Scheepjes Colour Crafter (100% Acrylic), DK/light worsted, 100g (300m/328yd), in the following shades:

Tynaarlo (1011); 6 balls (A)

Verviers (2017); 2 balls (B)

HOOKS

3.5mm crochet hook

4.5mm crochet hook

OTHER TOOLS AND MATERIALS

Approx. 60cm (24in) square backing fabric (do not cut to size until Assembly)

Stuffing (old pillows/quilts/fabric etc) or foam pieces

Sewing needle, thread and pins

PATTERN MULTIPLES

Pattern works to a multiple of 20 stitches + 2 stitches for the starting chain.

TENSION (GAUGE)

13 sts and 18 rows measure 10 x 10cm (4 x 4in) over patt on a 4.5mm hook.

FINISHED SIZE

Top panel measures approx. 52 x 52cm (20½ x 20½in) after blocking

Side panels measure approx. 52 x 22cm (20½ x 8⅝in)

Footstool measures approx. 52cm (20½in) wide, 52cm (20½in) deep, 22cm (8⅝in) high

---

Notes

This footstool is made up of six sections: a top panel worked in A and B, four side panels worked in A, and a fabric base. Once all the pieces are made they are crocheted together, then filled with stuffing or foam before the base is sewn on to finish.

Work with two strands of yarn held together throughout. For the top panel, you will be working with four strands (two of A and two of B), so be careful they do not get tangled.

INSTRUCTIONS

Top panel

Using 2 strands of A held together and a 4.5mm hook, ch62.

Row 1: 1dc in second ch from hook and in each ch to end, turn. (61 sts)

Rows 2 to 33: Now follow Sun Spot Throw patt, starting at Row 2 (using 2 strands of A) and finishing at end of Row 33, using 2 strands each of A and B as indicated. Do not fasten off B at end of Row 32.

Rows 34 to 98: Rep Rows 2 to 33 of Sun Spot Throw patt twice more, then rep Row 2 of Sun Spot Throw patt once more.

Fasten off and weave in ends, then block Top Panel to as near square shape as possible without over-stretching.

SIDE PANEL

(make 4)

Each side panel will measure as one edge of top panel.

Using 2 strands of A held together and a 4.5mm hook, ch31.

Row 1: 1dc in second ch from hook and in each ch to end, turn. (30 sts)

Row 2: Ch1 (does not count as st throughout), 1dc in each st to end, turn.

Rep Row 2 until first side panel measures same length as corresponding edge of top panel.

Fasten off, weave in ends.

Make other three side panels to match other three sides.

FABRIC BASE

Cut the backing fabric to the same size as the top panel plus 8cm (3in) extra on the width and length measurements.

ASSEMBLY

With RS facing out, pin a side panel to its corresponding top panel edge, ensuring corners line up exactly.

Using a 3.5mm hook, join 2 strands of A with a slst in one corner (working this stitch and all stitches through both side panel and top panel approx. 1cm (⅜in) in from edge). Ch1, work dc stitches along edge at regular intervals to join.

Rep to join each side panel to the top panel, and to join seams between side panels to make an open box.

Fasten off, weave in all ends.

Fill the footstool with stuffing so it is plump. Place the backing fabric RS out on top of the stuffing, tuck in the four edges, then whip stitch in place with a needle and thread.

TOP TIP

Turn this into an upcycling project by using any old cushions, quilts or spare fabric offcuts for the stuffing.

Hail Kale Throw

SKILL LEVEL:

My parents went in for the full self-sufficiency life back in the 1970s. They grew most of our vegetables and fruit, and my dad used to go hunting for meat. We even had hunting ferrets, which lived in the garden. Being young I, of course, wanted to bring the ferrets into the house and cuddle them and dress them up – until my dad pointed out they'd bite your fingers off. Not the ideal pets after all. I remember being made to eat a lot of greens. I mean a LOT. Hence Hail Kale Throw: my nod of respect to all the green veg that my parents forced my sister Emma and I to eat, to make us grow up big and strong.

YOU WILL NEED

YARN

Scheepjes Colour Crafter (100% Acrylic), DK/light worsted, 100g (300m/328yd), in the following shades:

Utrecht (1009); 5 balls (A)

Verviers (2017); 4 balls (B)

HOOK

5.5mm crochet hook

PATTERN MULTIPLES

Pattern works to a multiple of 20 sts + 6 sts for the starting chain.

TENSION (GAUGE)

15 sts and 18 rows measure 10 x 10cm (4 x 4in) over patt using a 5.5mm hook.

FINISHED SIZE

Approx. 99 x 150cm (39 x 59in) excluding tassels

Note

This throw is made up of five sections: Sections 1, 3 and 5 use A for the background, and B for the leaves. Sections 2 and 4 are simply a reverse of these colours. Once the main throw is finished, an edging is worked on each long side in A, and a row of tassels is added along each short edge in A for a leafy, frondy finish.

INSTRUCTIONS

Section 1

Using A, ch146.

Row 1 (RS): 1dc in second ch from hook and in each ch to end, turn. (145 sts)

Row 2 (WS): Ch1 (does not count as st throughout), 1dc in each st to end, cc to B, turn.

Row 3: Ch1, 1dc, ch2, skip 1 st, 3dc, ch8, skip 7 sts, 1dc, ch8, skip 7 sts, *5dc, ch8, skip 7 sts, 1dc, ch8, skip 7 sts; rep from * to last 5 sts, 3dc, ch2, skip 1 st, 1dc, turn.

Row 4: Ch1, 1dc, ch2, skip 2ch-sp, 3dc, ch8, skip 8ch-sp, 1dc, ch8, skip 8ch-sp, *5dc, ch8, skip 8ch-sp, 1dc, ch8, skip 8ch-sp; rep from * to last 5 sts, 3dc, ch2, skip 2ch-sp, 1dc, cc to A, turn.

Row 5: Ch1, 1dc, 1mtr, ch2, skip 1 st, *2dc, 7mtr, ch2, skip 1 st, 7mtr, 2dc, ch2, skip 1 st; rep from * to last 2 sts, 1mtr, 1dc, turn.

Row 6: Ch1, 2dc, ch2, skip 2ch-sp, *9dc, ch2, skip 2ch-sp; rep from * to last 2 sts, 2dc, cc, turn.

Row 7: Ch1, 1dc, ch2, skip 1 st, 1mtr, *ch5, skip 4 sts, 5dc, 1mtr, 5dc, ch5, skip 4 sts, 1mtr; rep from * to last 2 sts, ch2, skip 1 st, 1dc, turn.

Row 8: Ch1, 1dc, ch2, skip 2ch-sp, 1dc, *ch5, skip 5ch-sp, 11dc, ch5, skip 5ch-sp, 1dc; rep from * to last 2 sts, ch2, skip 2ch-sp, 1dc, cc, turn.

Row 9: Ch1, 1dc, 1mtr, 1dc, *4mtr, 5dc, ch2, skip 1 st, 5dc, 4mtr, 1dc; rep from * to last 2 sts, 1mtr, 1dc, turn.

Row 10: Ch1, 12dc, ch2, skip 2ch-sp, *19dc, ch2, skip 2ch-sp; rep from * to last 12 sts, 12dc, cc, turn.

Row 11: Ch1, 1dc, ch5, skip 4 sts, 7dc, 1mtr, 7dc, *ch6, skip 5 sts, 7dc, 1mtr, 7dc; rep from * to last 5 sts, ch5, skip 4 sts, 1dc, turn.

Row 12: Ch1, 1dc, ch5, skip 5ch-sp, 15dc, *ch6, skip 6ch-sp, 15dc; rep from * to last 5 sts, ch5, skip 5ch-sp, 1dc, cc, turn.

Row 13: Ch1, 1dc, 4mtr, 7dc, ch2, skip 1 st, 7dc, *5mtr, 7dc, ch2, skip 1 st, 7dc; rep from * to last 5 sts, 4mtr, 1dc, turn.

Row 14: As Row 10.

Row 15: Ch1, 1dc, ch5, skip 4 sts, 7dc, 1mtr, 7dc, *ch6, skip 5 sts, 7dc, 1mtr, 7dc; rep from * to last 5 sts, ch5, skip 4 sts, 1dc, turn.

Row 16: Ch1, 1dc, ch5, skip 5ch-sp, 15dc, *ch6, skip 6ch-sp, 15dc; rep from * to last 5 sts, ch5, skip 5ch-sp, 1dc, cc, turn.

Row 17: Ch1, 1dc, 4mtr, 7dc, ch2, skip 1 st, 7dc, *5mtr, 7dc, ch2, skip 1 st, 7dc; rep from * to last 5 sts, 4mtr, 1dc, turn.

Row 18: As Row 10.

Row 19: Ch1, 1dc, ch6, skip 5 sts, 6dc, 1mtr, 6dc, *ch8, skip 7 sts, 6dc, 1mtr, 6dc; rep from * to last 6 sts, ch6, skip 5 sts, 1dc, turn.

Row 20: Ch1, 1dc, ch6, skip 6ch-sp, 13dc, *ch8, skip 8ch-sp, 13dc; rep from * to last 6 sts, ch6, skip 6ch-sp, 1dc, cc, turn.

Row 21: Ch1, 1dc, 5mtr, 6dc, ch2, skip 1 st, 6dc, *7mtr, 6dc, ch2, skip 1 st, 6dc; rep from * to last 6 sts, 5mtr, 1dc, turn.

Row 22: As Row 10.

Row 23: Ch1, 1dc, ch2, skip 1 st, 1dc, *ch6, skip 5 sts, 4dc, 1mtr, 4dc, ch6, skip 5 sts, 1dc; rep from * to last 2 sts, ch2, skip 1 st, 1dc, turn.

Row 24: Ch1, 1dc, ch2, skip 2ch-sp, 1dc, *ch6, skip 6ch-sp, 9dc, ch6, skip 6ch-sp, 1dc; rep from * to last 2 sts, ch2, skip 2ch-sp, 1dc, cc, turn.

Row 25: Ch1, 1dc, 1mtr, ch2, skip 1 st, *5mtr, 4dc, ch2, skip 1 st, 4dc, 5mtr, ch2, skip 1 st; rep from * to last 2 sts, 1mtr, 1dc, turn.

Row 26: As Row 6.

Row 27: Ch1, 1dc, ch2, skip 1 st, 1mtr, *2dc, ch6, skip 5 sts, 2dc, 1mtr; rep from * to last 2 sts, ch2, skip 1 st, 1dc, turn.

Row 28: Ch1, 1dc, ch2, skip 2ch-sp, 3dc, ch6, skip 6ch-sp, *5dc, ch6, skip 6ch-sp; rep from * to last 5 sts, 3dc, ch2, skip 2ch-sp, 1dc, cc, turn.

Row 29: Ch1, 1dc, 1mtr, ch2, skip 1 st, *2dc, 5mtr, 2dc, ch2, skip 1 st; rep from * to last 2 sts, 1mtr, 1dc, turn.

Row 30: As Row 6.

Row 31: Ch1, 1dc, ch2, skip 1 st, 1mtr, *4dc, ch6, skip 5 sts, 1mtr, ch6, skip 5 sts, 4dc, 1mtr; rep from * to last 2 sts, ch2, skip 1 st, 1dc, turn.

Row 32: Ch1, 1dc, ch2, skip 2ch-sp, 5dc, ch6, skip 6ch-sp, 1dc, ch6, skip 6ch-sp, *9dc, ch6, skip 6ch-sp, 1dc, ch6, skip 6ch-sp; rep from * to last 7 sts, 5dc, ch2, skip 2ch-sp, 1dc, cc, turn.

Row 33: Ch1, 1dc, 1mtr, ch2, skip 1 st, *4dc, 5mtr, 1dc, 5mtr, 4dc, ch2, skip 1 st; rep from * to last 2 sts, 1mtr, 1dc, turn.

Row 34: Ch1, 2dc, ch2, skip 2ch-sp, *19dc, ch2, skip 2ch-sp; rep from * to last 2 sts, 2dc, cc, turn.

Row 35: Ch1, 1dc, ch2, skip 1 st, 1mtr, *6dc, ch8, skip 7 sts, 6dc, 1mtr; rep from * to last 2 sts, ch2, skip 1 st, 1dc, turn.

Row 36: Ch1, 1dc, ch2, skip 2ch-sp, 7dc, ch8, skip 8ch-sp, *13dc, ch8, skip 8ch-sp; rep from * to last 9 sts, 7dc, ch2, skip 2ch-sp, 1dc, cc, turn.

Row 37: Ch1, 1dc, 1mtr, ch2, skip 1 st, *6dc, 7mtr, 6dc, ch2, skip 1 st; rep from * to last 2 sts, 1mtr, 1dc, turn.

Row 38: As Row 34.

Row 39: Ch1, 1dc, ch2, skip 1 st, 1mtr, *7dc, ch6, skip 5 sts, 7dc, 1mtr; rep from * to last 2 sts, ch2, skip 1 st, 1dc, turn.

Row 40: Ch1, 1dc, ch2, skip 2ch-sp, 8dc, ch6, skip 6ch-sp, *15dc, ch6, skip 6ch-sp; rep from * to last 10 sts, 8dc, ch2, skip 2ch-sp, 1dc, cc, turn.

Row 41: Ch1, 1dc, 1mtr, ch2, skip 1 st, *7dc, 5mtr, 7dc, ch2, skip 1 st; rep from * to last 2 sts, 1mtr, 1dc, turn.

Row 42: As Row 34.

Row 43: Ch1, 1dc, ch2, skip 1 st, 1mtr, *7dc, ch6, skip 5 sts, 7dc, 1mtr; rep from * to last 2 sts, ch2, skip 1 st, 1dc, turn.

Row 44: Ch1, 1dc, ch2, skip 2ch-sp, 8dc, ch6, skip 6ch-sp, *15dc, ch6, skip 6ch-sp; rep from * to last 10 sts, 8dc, ch2, skip 2ch-sp, 1dc, cc, turn.

Row 45: Ch1, 1dc, 1mtr, ch2, skip 1 st, *7dc, 5mtr, 7dc, ch2, skip 1 st; rep from * to last 2 sts, 1mtr, 1dc, turn.

Row 46: As Row 34.

Row 47: Ch1, 1dc, ch2, skip 1 st, 1mtr, *5dc, ch5, skip 4 sts, 1dc, ch5, skip 4 sts, 5dc, 1mtr; rep from * to last 2 sts, ch2, skip 1 st, 1dc, turn.

Row 48: Ch1, 1dc, ch2, skip 2ch-sp, 6dc, ch5, skip 5ch-sp, 1dc, ch5, skip 5ch-sp, *11dc, ch5, skip 5ch-sp, 1dc, ch5, skip 5ch-sp; rep from * to last 8 sts, 6dc, ch2, skip 2ch-sp, 1dc, cc, turn.

Row 49: Ch1, 1dc, 1mtr, ch2, skip 1 st, *5dc, 4mtr, ch2, skip 1 st, 4mtr, 5dc, ch2, skip 1 st; rep from * to last 2 sts, 1mtr, 1dc, turn.

Row 50: Ch1, 2dc, ch2, skip 2ch-sp, *9dc, ch2, skip 2ch-sp; rep from * to last 2 sts, 2dc, cc, turn.

Row 51: Ch1, 1dc, ch2, skip 1 st, 1mtr, *ch8, skip 7 sts, 2dc, 1mtr, 2dc, ch8, skip 7sts, 1mtr; rep from * to last 2 sts, ch2, skip 1 st, 1dc, turn.

Row 52: Ch1, 1dc, ch2, skip 2ch-sp, 1dc, *ch8, skip 8ch-sp, 5dc, ch8, skip 8ch-sp, 1dc; rep from * to last 2 sts, ch2, skip 2ch-sp, 1dc, cc, turn.

Row 53: Ch1, 1dc, 1mtr, 1dc, *7mtr, 5dc, 7mtr, 1dc; rep from * to last 2 sts, 1mtr, 1dc, turn.

Row 54: Ch1, 1dc in each st to end, cc, turn.

Do not fasten off yarns.

Section 2

Row 1 (RS): Using B, ch1, 1dc in each st to end, turn. (145 sts)

Row 2 (WS): Ch1, 1dc in each st to end, cc to A, turn.

Rows 3 to 54: As Rows 3 to 54 of Section 1, using A where B is indicated, and B where A is indicated.

Section 3

Row 1 (RS): Using A, ch1, 1dc in each st to end, turn. (145 sts)

Row 2 (WS): Ch1, 1dc in each st to end, cc to B, turn.

Rows 3 to 54: As Rows 3 to 54 of Section 1.

Sections 4 and 5: As Sections 2 and 3, fasten off B at end of Section 5, do not fasten off A.

EDGING

Edging is worked along two long sides only.

Edge first long side

Row 1 (WS): Using A and with WS facing, ch1, rotate work 90 degrees and work along first long side as follows: *1dc in each of next four row ends, *skip next row end; rep from * to end, finishing on any st in rep. If the last st happens to be a skipped st, just make 1dc to finish the row. Turn.

Row 2 (RS): Ch1, 1dc in each st to end.

Fasten off and weave in ends.

Edge second long side

Row 1 (WS): With WS facing, join A with a slst in first row end on other long side, ch1, 1dc in same st, 1dc in each of next three row ends, *skip next row end, 1dc in each of next 4 row ends; rep from * to end, finishing on any st in rep. If the last st happens to be a skipped st, just make 1dc to finish the row. Turn.

Row 2 (RS): Ch1, 1dc in each st to end, turn.

Fasten off and weave in ends.

TASSELS

(make approx. 50 per short side, or as many as you like)

Cut five 20cm (8in) lengths of A, hold them together and fold them in half, poke the looped end a short way through the first stitch at the end of a short side of the throw. Take the cut ends of yarn and thread them through the loop, then pull them gently all the way through to secure the tassel. Repeat every three stitches along each short end. Trim the ends to neaten up.

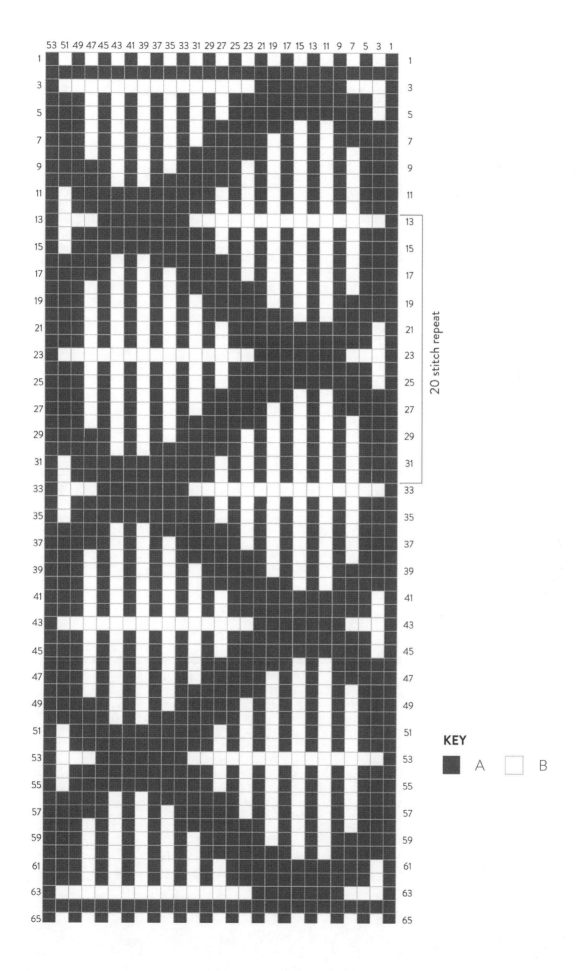

Each square represents a stitch.

To work from this chart, rotate it by 90 degrees clockwise. Read all odd-numbered (RS) rows from right to left, and all even-numbered (WS) rows from left to right.

Work rows 1 to 54 five times, switching A and B for second and fourth repeats.

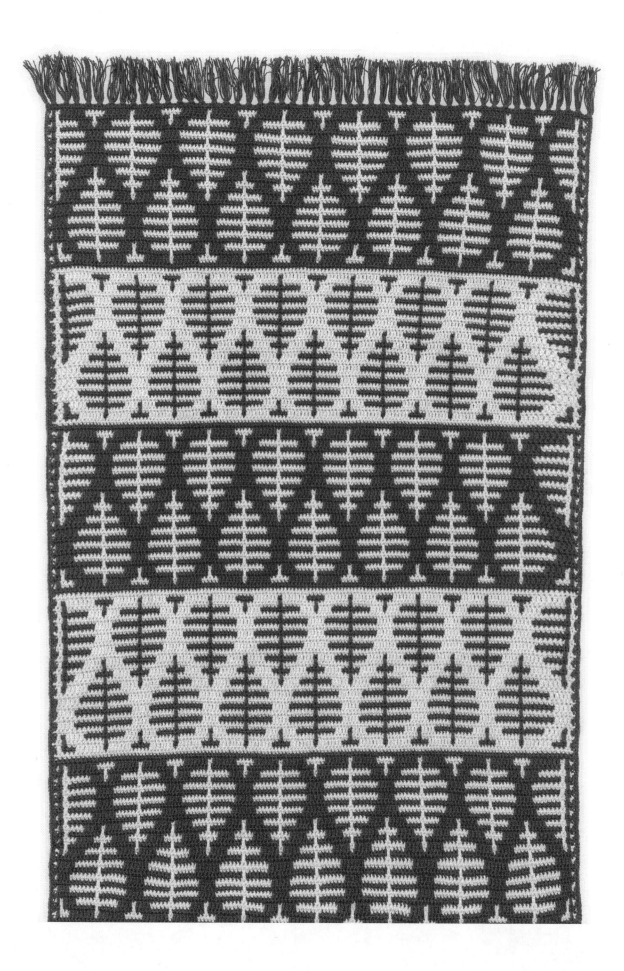

TOP TIP

This would make a gorgeous autumn shawl! Simply adjust the starting chain and choose a fine yarn in muted woodland colours.

Try a new colourway

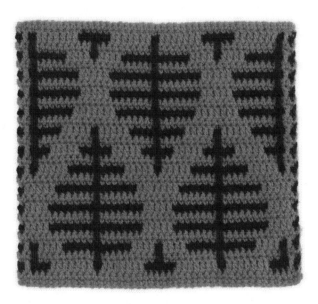

COLOURS OF NATURE

Let Mother Nature be your guide and look to the seasons for inspiration. Autumn has definitely arrived here, with gorgeous leaf-turning shades of vibrant orange and deep red.

SPIN-OFF PROJECT:
Leafy Table Runner

SKILL LEVEL:

I love the simplicity of this Scandi-inspired table runner; the way the leaves interlock with each other is very calming and pleasing somehow. I kept the colours neutral to show off the beautiful pattern, but I can see myself getting twitchy when people put glasses of red wine anywhere near it! Working with jute yarn is wonderful, but it needs patience as it doesn't 'give' in the same way as other yarns. But worth the effort (and the sore fingers) I think!

YOU WILL NEED

YARN

Scheepjes Mighty (32% jute/68% cotton), 4-ply/sport, 50g (80m/87yds), in the following shades:

Canyon (759); 6 balls (A)

Mountain (755); 6 balls (B)

HOOK

4mm crochet hook

OTHER TOOLS

Stitch markers

PATTERN MULTIPLES

Pattern works to a multiple of 20 stitches + 6 stitches for the starting chain.

TENSION (GAUGE)

15 sts and 20 rows measure 10 x 10cm (4 x 4in) over patt using a 4mm hook.

FINISHED SIZE

Approx. 31 x 168cm (12¼ x 66in)

Note

This table runner has a very long starting chain: place stitch markers every 50 stitches in your chain to mark your place just in case you lose count. Once the main panel is made, it is edged in B along the short ends to finish. If you don't like the more open 'rustic look' of this design, go down a hook size for a tighter finish. You can adjust your starting chain (see Pattern Multiples) to fit your dining table.

INSTRUCTIONS

Using B, ch246.

Row 1 (RS): 1dc in second ch from hook and in each ch to end, turn. (245 sts)

Rows 2 to 4: Ch1 (does not count as st throughout), 1dc in each st to end, turn. Cc to A at end of Row 4.

Row 5: Ch1, 1dc in each st to end, turn.

Now follow Section 1 of Hail Kale Throw patt, starting at Row 2 (using A), and finishing at end of Row 54, using A and B as indicated. Cc to B at end of Row 54.

Fasten off A.

Next 4 rows: Using B, ch1, 1dc in each st to end, turn.

Do not fasten off B.

Weave in all ends before edging.

EDGING

Edging is worked along two short sides only.

Edge first short side

Using B and with WS facing, rotate work 90 degrees to work along first short edge.

Row 1 (WS): Ch1, *1dc in each of next four row ends, skip next row end; rep from * to end, finishing on any st in rep. If last st happens to be a skipped st, just make 1dc to finish row. Turn.

Rows 2 to 4: Ch1, 1dc in each st to end, turn.

Fasten off at end of Row 4, weave in ends.

Edge second short side

Row 1 (WS): Join B with a slst in first row end on other short side, ch1, 1dc in same st, 1dc in each of next three row ends, *skip next row end, 1dc in each of next four row ends; rep from * to end, finishing on any st in rep. If last st happens to be a skipped st, just make 1dc to finish row.

Rows 2 to 4: Ch1, 1dc in each st to end, turn.

Fasten off at end of Row 4 and weave in ends.

TOP TIP

Washable yarn might be a good idea just in case the red wine makes an appearance!

Into the Trees Throw

These trees seem to stretch away endlessly into the distance, don't they? Forests are truly magical and mysterious places, full of whispers and shadows and spirits… or is that just my imagination playing tricks? I love the idea of wandering off the track and getting lost in a forest of beautiful misty blue and rusty orange. Maybe the reality would be rather less appealing when night falls, but the idea is fun when I'm safe and sound at home! This is a super luxurious throw, heavy and cosy, thanks to the beautiful Namaste yarn.

YOU WILL NEED

YARN

Scheepjes Namaste (50% virgin wool/50% acrylic), chunky/bulky 100g (85m/93yds), in the following shades:

Scale (625); 8 balls (A)

Gate (618); 9 balls (B)

HOOK

8mm crochet hook

PATTERN MULTIPLES

Pattern works to a multiple of 10 stitches + 6 stitches for the starting chain.

TENSION (GAUGE)

10 sts and 12 rows measure 10 x 10cm (4 x 4in) over patt using an 8mm hook.

FINISHED SIZE

Approx. 97 x 123cm (38¼ x 48½in)

Note

Just two yarns are used here – the misty blue of A makes a background to the rusty orange trees in B. Once the main throw is made it is edged in B, then 11 tassels in B are added along each short end as a finishing touch.

INSTRUCTIONS

Using A, ch96.

Row 1 (RS): 1dc in second ch from hook and in each ch to end, turn. (95 sts)

Row 2 (WS): Ch1 (does not count as st throughout), 1dc in each st to end, cc to B, turn.

Row 3: Ch1, 1dc, ch2, skip 1 st, 1dc, *ch5, skip 4 sts, 1dc; rep from * to last 2 sts, ch2, skip 1 st, 1dc, turn.

Row 4: Ch1, 1dc, ch2, skip 2ch-sp, 1dc, *ch5, skip 5ch-sp, 1dc; rep from * to last 2 sts, ch2, skip 2ch-sp, 1dc, cc to A, turn.

Row 5: Ch1, 1dc, 1mtr, ch2, skip 1 st, *4mtr, 1dc, 4mtr, ch2, skip 1 st; rep from * to last 2 sts, 1mtr, 1dc, turn.

Row 6: Ch1, 2dc, ch2, skip 2ch-sp, *9dc, ch2, skip 2ch-sp; rep from * to last 2 sts, 2dc, cc, turn.

Row 7: Ch1, 1dc, ch2, skip 1 st, 1mtr, *4dc, ch2, skip 1 st, 4dc, 1mtr; rep from * to last 2 sts, ch2, skip 1 st, 1dc, turn.

Row 8: Ch1, 1dc, ch2, skip 2ch-sp, 5dc, ch2, skip 2ch-sp, *9dc, ch2, skip 2ch-sp; rep from * to last 7 sts, 5dc, ch2, skip 2ch-sp, 1dc, cc, turn.

Row 9: Ch1, 1dc, 1mtr, ch2, skip 1 st, *4dc, 1mtr, 4dc, ch2, skip 1 st; rep from * to last 2 sts, 1mtr, 1dc, turn.

Row 10: Ch1, 2dc, ch2, skip 2ch-sp, *9dc, ch2, skip 2ch-sp; rep from * to last 2 sts, 2dc, cc, turn.

Row 11: Ch1, 1dc, ch2, skip 1 st, 1mtr, *3dc, ch4, skip 3 sts, 3dc, 1mtr; rep from * to last 2 sts, ch2, skip 1 st, 1dc, turn.

Row 12: Ch1, 1dc, ch2, skip 2ch-sp, 4dc, ch4, skip 4ch-sp, *7dc, ch4, skip 4ch-sp; rep from * to last 6 sts, 4dc, ch2, skip 2ch-sp, 1dc, cc, turn.

Row 13: Ch1, 1dc, 1mtr, ch2, skip 1 st, *3dc, 3mtr, 3dc, ch2, skip 1 st; rep from * to last 2 sts, 1mtr, 1dc, turn.

Row 14: Ch1, 2dc, ch2, skip 2ch-sp, *9dc, ch2, skip 2ch-sp; rep from * to last 2 sts, 2dc, cc, turn.

Row 15: Ch1, 1dc, ch2, skip 1 st, 1mtr, *2dc, ch6, skip 5 sts, 2dc, 1mtr; rep from * to last 2 sts, ch2, skip 1 st, 1dc, turn.

Row 16: Ch1, 1dc, ch2, skip 2ch-sp, 3dc, ch6, skip 6ch-sp, *5dc, ch6, skip 6ch-sp; rep from * to last 5 sts, 3dc, ch2, skip 2ch-sp, 1dc, cc, turn.

Row 17: Ch1, 1dc, 1mtr, ch2, skip 1 st, *2dc, 5mtr, 2dc, ch2, skip 1 st; rep from * to last 2 sts, 1mtr, 1dc, turn.

Row 18: Ch1, 2dc, ch2, skip 2ch-sp, *9dc, ch2, skip 2ch-sp; rep from * to last 2 sts, 2dc, cc, turn.

Row 19: Ch1, 1dc, ch2, skip 1 st, 1mtr, *1dc, ch8, skip 7 sts, 1dc, 1mtr; rep from * to last 2 sts, ch2, skip 1 st, 1dc, turn.

Row 20: Ch1, 1dc, ch2, skip 2ch-sp, 2dc, ch8, skip 8ch-sp, *3dc, ch8, skip 8ch-sp; rep from * to last 4 sts, 2dc, ch2, skip 2ch-sp, 1dc, cc, turn.

Row 21: Ch1, 1dc, 1mtr, ch2, skip 1 st, *1dc, 7mtr, 1dc, ch2, skip 1 st; rep from * to last 2 sts, 1mtr, 1dc, turn.

Row 22: Ch1, 2dc, ch2, skip 2ch-sp, *9dc, ch2, skip 2ch-sp; rep from * to last 2 sts, 2dc, cc, turn.

Row 23: Ch1, 1dc, ch2, skip 1 st, 1mtr, *ch5, skip 4 sts, 1dc, ch5, skip 4 sts, 1mtr; rep from * to last 2 sts, ch2, skip 1 st, 1dc, turn.

Row 24: Ch1, 1dc, ch2, skip 2ch-sp, 1dc, *ch5, skip 5ch-sp, 1dc; rep from * to last 2 sts, ch2, skip 2ch-sp, 1dc, cc, turn.

Row 25: Ch1, 1dc, 1mtr, 1dc, *4mtr, ch2, skip 1 st, 4mtr, 1dc; rep from * to last 2 sts, 1mtr, 1dc, turn.

Row 26: Ch1, 7dc, ch2, skip 2ch-sp, *9dc, ch2, skip 2ch-sp; rep from * to last 7 sts, 7dc, cc, turn.

Row 27: Ch1, 1dc, ch3, skip 2 sts, 4dc, 1mtr, *4dc, ch2, skip 1 st, 4dc, 1mtr; rep from * to last 7 sts, 4dc, ch3, skip 2 sts, 1dc, turn.

Row 28: Ch1, 1dc, ch3, skip 3ch-sp, 9dc, *ch2, skip 2ch-sp, 9dc; rep from * to last 3 sts, ch3, skip 3ch-sp, 1dc, cc, turn.

Row 29: Ch1, 1dc, 2mtr, *4dc, ch2, skip 1 st, 4dc, 1mtr; rep from * to last 2 sts, 1mtr, 1dc, turn.

Row 30: Ch1, 7dc, ch2, skip 2ch-sp, *9dc, ch2, skip 2ch-sp; rep from * to last 7 sts, 7dc, cc, turn.

Row 31: Ch1, 1dc, *ch4, skip 3 sts, 3dc, 1mtr, 3dc; rep from * to last 4 sts, ch4, skip 3 sts, 1dc, turn.

Row 32: Ch1, 1dc, *ch4, skip 4ch-sp, 7dc; rep from * to last 4 sts, ch4, skip 4ch-sp, 1dc, cc, turn.

Row 33: Ch1, 1dc, *3mtr, 3dc, ch2, skip 1 st, 3dc; rep from * to last 4 sts, 3mtr, 1dc, turn.

Row 34: Ch1, 7dc, ch2, skip 2ch-sp, *9dc, ch2, skip 2ch-sp; rep from * to last 7 sts, 7dc, cc, turn.

Row 35: Ch1, 1dc, ch5, skip 4 sts, 2dc, 1mtr, 2dc, *ch6, skip 5 sts, 2dc, 1mtr, 2dc; rep from * to last 5 sts, ch5, skip 4 sts, 1dc, turn.

Row 36: Ch1, 1dc, ch5, skip 5ch-sp, 5dc, *ch6, skip 6ch-sp, 5dc; rep from * to last 5 sts, ch5, skip 5ch-sp, 1dc, cc, turn.

Row 37: Ch1, 1dc, 4mtr, 2dc, ch2, skip 1 st, 2dc, *5mtr, 2dc, ch2, skip 1 st, 2dc; rep from * to last 5 sts, 4mtr, 1dc, turn.

Row 38: Ch1, 7dc, ch2, skip 2ch-sp, *9dc, ch2, skip 2ch-sp; rep from * to last 7 sts, 7dc, cc, turn.

Row 39: Ch1, 1dc, ch6, skip 5 sts, 1dc, 1mtr, 1dc, *ch8, skip 7 sts, 1dc, 1mtr, 1dc; rep from * to last 6 sts, ch6, skip 5 sts, 1dc, turn.

Row 40: Ch1, 1dc, ch6, skip 6ch-sp, 3dc, *ch8, skip 8ch-sp, 3dc; rep from * to last 6 sts, ch6, skip 6ch-sp, 1dc, cc, turn.

Row 41: Ch1, 1dc, 5mtr, 1dc, ch2, skip 1 st, 1dc, *7mtr, 1dc, ch2, skip 1 st, 1dc; rep from * to last 6 sts, 5mtr, 1dc, turn.

Row 42: Ch1, 7dc, ch2, skip 2ch-sp, *9dc, ch2, skip 2ch-sp; rep from * to last 7 sts, 7dc, cc, turn.

Row 43: Ch1, 1dc, ch2, skip 1 st, 1dc, *ch5, skip 4 sts, 1mtr, ch5, skip 4 sts, 1dc; rep from * to last 2 sts, ch2, skip 1 st, 1dc, turn.

Row 44: Ch1, 1dc, ch2, skip 2ch-sp, 1dc, *ch5, skip 5ch-sp, 1dc; rep from * to last 2 sts, ch2, skip 2ch-sp, 1dc, cc, turn.

Rows 45 to 144: Rep Rows 5 to 44 twice more, then rep Rows 5 to 24 once more.

Row 145: Ch1, 1dc, 1mtr, 1dc, *4mtr, 1dc; rep from * to last 2 sts, 1mtr, 1dc, turn.

Row 146: Ch1, 1dc in each st to end.

Fasten off yarns and weave in ends.

EDGING

Work with RS facing throughout.

Round 1 (RS): Join B with slst in top right hand st, ch1, (1dc, ch2, 1dc) in same st, 1dc in each st to last st on top edge, (1dc, ch2, 1dc) in last st, rotate work 90 degrees, 1dc in each of next three row ends, *skip next row end, 1dc in each of next four row ends; rep from * to end of long side, finishing on any st in rep, (1dc, ch2, 1dc) in first st on bottom edge, 1dc in each st along to last st on bottom edge, (1dc, ch2, 1dc) in last st, rotate work 90 degrees, 1dc in each of next three row ends, **skip next row end, 1dc in each of next four row ends; rep from ** to end of long side, finishing on any st in rep, slst to beg dc.

Round 2: Ch3 (counts as 1 tr) *1tr in next st and in each st to 2ch-sp, (1tr, ch2, 1tr) in ch-sp; rep from * around to end, slst to top of beg ch-3.

Round 3: Ch1, 1dc in same st, *1dc in each st to 2ch-sp, (1dc, ch2, 1dc) in ch-sp; rep from * around to end, slst to beg dc.

Fasten off and weave in ends.

TASSELS

(make 22)

Wrap B about 16 times around a piece of card approx. 10cm (4in) in length. Insert a 30cm (12in) length of B under all the loops at the top, knot tightly to fasten and secure the loops together. Cut through all the loops along the bottom edge. Wind another 30cm (12cm) piece of B three times around all the strands (except the joining yarn at the top) approx. 3cm (1⅛in) from the top. Knot to secure. Trim the tassel to level off.

Attach the tassels along each short end as follows: one at each corner, then the remaining nine so they line up with each dot between the trees. Use the joining yarn at the top of each tassel to knot securely to the edge. Weave in all ends.

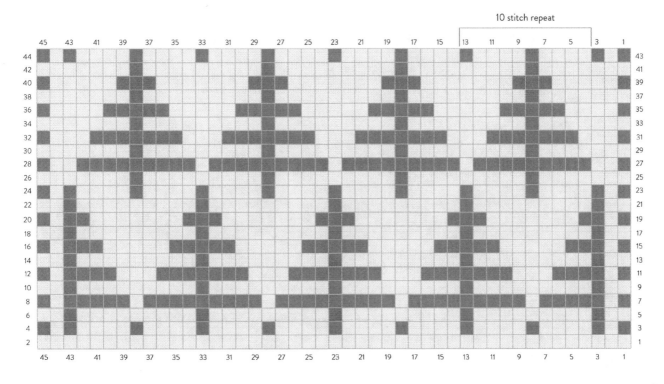

KEY

A ◼ B

Each square represents a stitch.

Read all odd-numbered (RS) rows from right to left, and all even-numbered (WS) rows from left to right.

Work rows 1 to 44 to start, and on subsequent repeats work rows 5 to 44.

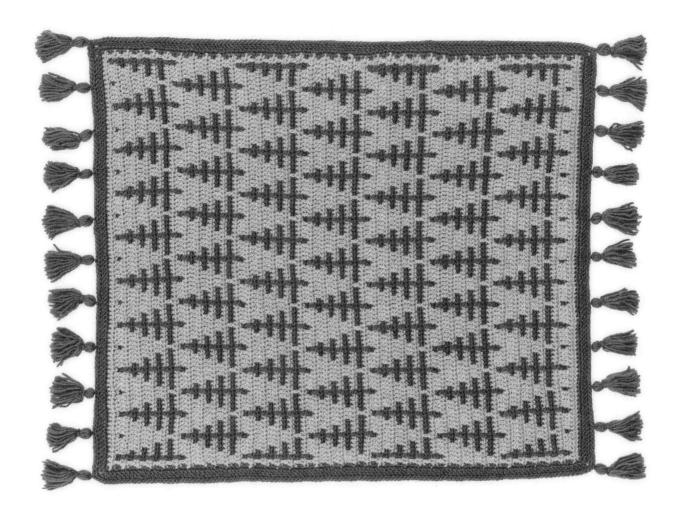

TOP TIP

A lovely project to make in the winter as it will keep your knees cosy while you crochet.

Try a new colourway

PLAY WITH OMBRÉ

There are many beautiful ombré yarns out there, but it's easy to create your own ombré destiny. These tones of grey-blue (almost like a little monochrome rainbow) on a moss-green background make a cool and fresh forest scene.

SPIN-OFF PROJECT:
Evergreen Vases

I do love the hunkering down aspect of winter – celebrating the season by lighting candles and bringing evergreen foliage into the house. And, of course, the odd sherry by the fire, to keep spirits up during the dark evenings. Mother Nature is just resting and preparing herself for spring, so there's much to be thankful for, and to look forward to. These forest-inspired vases look so pretty filled with whatever beautiful sprigs and green loveliness my garden can offer.

YOU WILL NEED

YARN

Scheepjes Linen Soft (27% linen/47% cotton/26% acrylic), DK/light worsted, 50g (135m/147yds), in the following shades:

Bright green (606); 1 ball (A)

Off-white (616); 1 ball (B)

Dark green (605); 1 ball (C)

HOOK

3mm crochet hook

OTHER TOOLS AND MATERIALS

Two glass jars or any suitable receptacle, 32cm (12½in) circumference, 14cm (5½in) high

Needle and thread

PATTERN MULTIPLES

Pattern works to a multiple of 10 stitches + 6 stitches for the starting chain.

TENSION (GAUGE)

16 sts and 23 rows measure 10 x 10cm (4 x 4in) over patt using a 3mm hook.

FINISHED SIZE

Approx. 13 x 35cm (5 x 13¾in) laid flat

Notes

Each cover is a simple rectangle, worked from the bottom up, then sewn closed along the back seam to form a tube. To ensure a good fit, make a starting chain to fit just around the circumference of the jar (using the Pattern Multiples). The finished cover should be slightly wider than the jar circumference as it will be overlapped before sewing. To adjust the height, either add more rows of C at the bottom and top or, to cover a much bigger receptacle, follow the full Into The Trees Throw pattern to make two rows of trees.

Use A, B and C as indicated to make the first cover, then switch A and C around for the second one, using A where C is indicated, and vice versa.

INSTRUCTIONS

Using C, ch66.

Foundation row 1 (RS): 1dc in second ch from hook and in each ch to end, turn. (65 sts)

Foundation row 2: Ch1 (does not count as st), 1dc in each st to end, turn. Cc to A, fasten off C.

Main pattern

Row 1 (RS): Using A, ch1 (does not count as st throughout), 1dc in each st to end, turn. (65 sts)

Rows 2 to 24: Now follow Into The Trees Throw patt, starting at Row 2 (using A) and finishing at end of Row 24, using A and B as indicated.

Fasten off B, keep A attached.

Row 25: Ch1, 1dc, 1mtr, 1dc, *4mtr, 1dc; rep from * to last 2 sts, 1mtr, 1dc, turn.

Row 26: Ch1, 1dc in each st to end, cc to C, fasten off A and B.

Rows 27 to 28: Ch1, 1dc in each st to end, turn.

Row 29: Ch1, 1slst in each st to end to make a neat top edge.

Fasten off and weave in ends.

Make the second cover in the same way, using C where A is indicated, and A where C is indicated for the other colourway.

ASSEMBLY

Wrap the finished cover around the jar, overlapping it to fit. With a needle and thread, sew down the back seam with tiny whip stitches.

Fasten off.

TOP TIP

This is a great way to upcycle any old jars or tins. It's also a great stash buster; use any spare bits and pieces of yarn.

Dutch Houses Throw

SKILL LEVEL:

I've always loved getting totally and utterly lost in cities, wandering around without a clue where I am, soaking up the vibes. It was so easy to do in the 'old days' before mobile phones came along with their sensible maps. Cities offer some of their best secrets if you look up, don't they? Of course, you've got to watch out for traffic and irate pedestrians who shout 'tourist' at you as you blunder around, marvelling at a particularly lovely stepped gable. These Dutch houses remind me of wonderful trips to the Netherlands; I've been a few times recently to meet up with the fabulous Scheepjes team and enjoy a cheese fondue or two in extremely good company.

YOU WILL NEED

YARN

Scheepjes Colour Crafter (100% Acrylic), DK/light worsted, 100g (300m/328yds), in the following shades:

Sint Niklaas (2019); 5 Balls (A)

Leek (1132); 2 balls (B)

Eelde (1422); 2 balls (C)

Dordrecht (1062); 1 ball (D)

Pollare (2018); 1 ball (E)

HOOK

5.5mm crochet hook

PATTERN MULTIPLES

Pattern works to a multiple of 28 stitches + 22 stitches for the starting chain.

TENSION (GAUGE)

15 sts and 18 rows measure 10 x 10cm (4 x 4in) over patt using a 5.5mm hook.

FINISHED SIZE

Approx. 90 x 160cm (35⅜ x 63in)

Note

Keep A attached throughout as the background colour. Five 'streets' of houses are made in the following yarn sequence: B, C, D, C, B. Join each new yarn at the start of every Row 5 repeat and fasten it off at the end of every Row 58 repeat. A simple edging in E is added to finish.

INSTRUCTIONS

Using A, ch134.

Row 1 (RS): 1dc in second ch from hook and in each ch to end, turn. (133 sts)

Rows 2 to 4: Ch1 (does not count as st throughout), 1dc in each st to end, turn. Cc to B at end of Row 4.

Row 5: Ch1, 1dc, ch4, skip 3 sts, 13dc, *ch2, skip 1 st, 13dc; rep from * to last 4 sts, ch4, skip 3 sts, 1dc, turn.

Row 6: Ch1, 1dc, ch4, skip 4ch-sp, 13dc, *ch2, skip 2ch-sp, 13dc; rep from * to last 4 sts, ch4, skip 4ch-sp, 1dc, cc to A, turn.

Row 7: Ch1, 1dc, 3mtr, ch6, skip 5 sts, 3dc, ch6, skip 5 sts, *1mtr, ch3, skip 2 sts, 4dc, ch2, skip 1 st, 4dc, ch3, skip 2 sts, 1mtr, ch6, skip 5 sts, 3dc, ch6, skip 5 sts; rep from * to last 4 sts, 3mtr, 1dc, turn.

Row 8: Ch1, 4dc, ch6, skip 6ch-sp, 3dc, ch6, skip 6ch-sp, *1dc, ch3, skip 3ch-sp, 4dc, ch2, skip 2ch-sp, 4dc, ch3, skip 3ch-sp, 1dc, ch6, skip 6ch-sp, 3dc, ch6, skip 6ch-sp; rep from * to last 4 sts, 4dc, cc, turn.

Row 9: Ch1, 1dc, [ch4, skip 3 sts, 5mtr] twice, *ch2, skip 1 st, 2mtr, ch5, skip 4 sts, 1mtr, ch5, skip 4 sts, 2mtr, ch2, skip 1 st, 5mtr, ch4, skip 3 sts, 5mtr; rep from * to last 4 sts, ch4, skip 3 sts, 1dc, turn.

Row 10: Ch1, 1dc, [ch4, skip 4ch-sp, 5dc] twice, *ch2, skip 2ch-sp, 2dc, ch5, skip 5ch-sp, 1dc, ch5, skip 5ch-sp, 2dc, ch2, skip 2ch-sp, 5dc, ch4, skip 4ch-sp, 5dc; rep from * to last 4 sts, ch4, skip 4ch-sp, 1dc, cc, turn.

Row 11: Ch1, 1dc, [3mtr, ch2, skip 1 st, 3dc, ch2, skip 1 st] twice, *1mtr, ch3, skip 2 sts, 4mtr, ch2, skip 1 st, 4mtr, ch3, skip 2 sts, 1mtr, ch2, skip 1 st, 3dc, ch2, skip 1 st, 3mtr, ch2, skip 1 st, 3dc, ch2, skip 1 st; rep from * to last 4 sts, 3mtr, 1dc, turn.

Row 12: Ch1, 4dc, [ch2, skip 2ch-sp, 3dc] 3 times, ch2, skip 2ch-sp, *1dc, ch3, skip 3ch-sp, 4dc, ch2, skip 2ch-sp, 4dc, ch3, skip 3ch-sp, 1dc, [ch2, skip 2ch-sp, 3dc] 3 times, ch2, skip 2ch-sp; rep from * to last 4 sts, 4dc, cc, turn.

Row 13: Ch1, 1dc, [ch4, skip 3 sts, 1mtr] 4 times, *ch2, skip 1 st, 2mtr, ch5, skip 4 sts, 1mtr, ch5, skip 4 sts, 2mtr, ch2, skip 1 st, [1mtr, ch4, skip 3 sts] 3 times, 1mtr; rep from * to last 4 sts, ch4, skip 3 sts, 1dc, turn.

Row 14: Ch1, 1dc, [ch4, skip 4ch-sp, 1dc] 4 times, *ch2, skip 2ch-sp, 2dc, ch5, skip 5ch-sp, 1dc, ch5, skip 5ch-sp, 2dc, ch2, skip 2ch-sp, [1dc, ch4, skip 4ch-sp] 3 times, 1dc; rep from * to last 4 sts, ch4, skip 4ch-sp, 1dc, cc, turn.

Row 15: Ch1, 1dc, [3mtr, ch2, skip 1 st] 4 times, *1mtr, ch3, skip 2 sts, 4mtr, ch2, skip 1 st, 4mtr, ch3, skip 2 sts, 1mtr, [ch2, skip 1 st, 3mtr] 3 times, ch2, skip 1 st; rep from * to last 4 sts, 3mtr, 1dc, turn.

Row 16: Ch1, 4dc, [ch2, skip 2ch-sp, 3dc] 3 times, ch2, skip 2ch-sp, *1dc, ch3, skip 3ch-sp, 4dc, ch2, skip 2ch-sp, 4dc, ch3, skip 3ch-sp, 1dc, [ch2, skip 2ch-sp, 3dc] 3 times, ch2, skip 2ch-sp; rep from * to last 4 sts, 4dc, cc, turn.

Row 17: Ch1, 1dc, ch4, skip 3 sts, [1mtr, 3dc] 3 times, 1mtr, *ch2, skip 1 st, 2mtr, 4dc, 1mtr, 4dc, 2mtr, ch2, skip 1 st, [1mtr, 3dc] 3 times, 1mtr; rep from * to last 4 sts, ch4, skip 3 sts, 1dc, turn.

Row 18: Ch1, 1dc, ch4, skip 4ch-sp, 13dc, *ch2, skip 2ch-sp, 13dc; rep from * to last 4 sts, ch4, skip 4ch-sp, 1dc, cc, turn.

Row 19: Ch1, 1dc, 3mtr, [ch2, skip 1 st, 3dc] 3 times, ch2, skip 1 st, *1mtr, ch3, skip 2 sts, 2dc, ch2, skip 1 st, 3dc, ch2, skip 1 st, 2dc, ch3, skip 2 sts, 1mtr, [ch2, skip 1 st, 3dc] 3 times, ch2, skip 1 st; rep from * to last 4 sts, 3mtr, 1dc, turn.

Row 20: Ch1, 4dc, [ch2, skip 2ch-sp, 3dc] 3 times, ch2, skip 2ch-sp, *1dc, ch3, skip 3ch-sp, 2dc, ch2, skip 2ch-sp, 3dc, ch2, skip 2ch-sp, 2dc, ch3, skip 3ch-sp, 1dc, [ch2, skip 2ch-sp, 3dc] 3 times, ch2, skip 2ch-sp; rep from * to last 4 sts, 4dc, cc, turn.

Row 21: Ch1, 1dc, [ch4, skip 3 sts, 1mtr] 4 times, *ch2, skip 1 st, 2mtr, ch3, skip 2 sts, 1mtr, ch4, skip 3 sts, 1mtr, ch3, skip 2 sts, 2mtr, ch2, skip 1 st, [1mtr, ch4, skip 3 sts] 3 times, 1mtr; rep from * to last 4 sts, ch4, skip 3 sts, 1dc, turn.

Row 22: Ch1, [1dc, ch4, skip 4ch-sp] 4 times, 1dc, *ch2, skip 2ch-sp, 2dc, ch3, skip 3ch-sp, 1dc, ch4, skip 4ch-sp, 1dc, ch3, skip 3ch-sp, 2dc, ch2, skip 2ch-sp, [1dc, ch4, skip 4ch-sp] 3 times, 1dc; rep from * to last 4 sts, ch4, skip 4ch-sp, 1dc, cc, turn.

Row 23: Ch1, 1dc, [3mtr, ch2, skip 1 st] 4 times, *1mtr, ch3, skip 2 sts, 2mtr, ch2, skip 1 st, 3mtr, ch2, skip 1 st, 2mtr, ch3, skip 2 sts, 1mtr, [ch2, skip 1 st, 3mtr] 3 times, ch2, skip 1 st; rep from * to last 4 sts, 3mtr, 1dc, turn.

Row 24: Ch1, 4dc, [ch2, skip 2ch-sp, 3dc] 3 times, ch2, skip 2ch-sp, *1dc, ch3, skip 3ch-sp, 2dc, ch2, skip 2ch-sp, 3dc, ch2, skip 2ch-sp, 2dc, ch3, skip 3ch-sp, 1dc, [ch2, skip 2ch-sp, 3dc] 3 times, ch2, skip 2ch-sp; rep from * to last 4 sts, 4dc, cc, turn.

Row 25: Ch1, 1dc, [ch4, skip 3 sts, 1mtr] 4 times, *ch2, skip 1 st, 2mtr, ch3, skip 2 sts, 1mtr, ch4, skip 3 sts, 1mtr, ch3, skip 2 sts, 2mtr, ch2, skip 1 st, [1mtr, ch4, skip 3 sts] 3 times, 1mtr; rep from * to last 4 sts, ch4, skip 3 sts, 1dc, turn.

Row 26: Ch1, [1dc, ch4, skip 4ch-sp] 4 times, 1dc, *ch2, skip 2ch-sp, 2dc, ch3, skip 3ch-sp, 1dc, ch4, skip 4ch-sp, 1dc, ch3, skip 3ch-sp, 2dc, ch2, skip 2ch-sp, [1dc, ch4, skip 4ch-sp] 3 times, 1dc; rep from * to last 4 sts, ch4, skip 4ch-sp, 1dc, cc, turn.

Row 27: Ch1, 1dc, [3mtr, ch2, skip 1 st] 4 times, *1mtr, ch3, skip 2 sts, 2mtr, ch2, skip 1 st, 3mtr, ch2, skip 1 st, 2mtr, ch3, skip 2 sts, 1mtr, [ch2, skip 1 st, 3mtr] 3 times, ch2, skip 1 st; rep from * to last 4 sts, 3mtr, 1dc, turn.

Row 28: Ch1, 4dc, [ch2, skip 2ch-sp, 3dc] 3 times, ch2, skip 2ch-sp, *1dc, ch3, skip 3ch-sp, 2dc, ch2, skip 2ch-sp, 3dc, ch2, skip 2ch-sp, 2dc, ch3, skip 3ch-sp, 1dc, [ch2, skip 2ch-sp, 3dc] 3 times, ch2, skip 2ch-sp; rep from * to last 4 sts, 4dc, cc, turn.

Row 29: Ch1, 1dc, ch4, skip 3 sts, [1mtr, 3dc] 3 times, 1mtr, *ch2, skip 1 st, 2mtr, 2dc, 1mtr, 3dc, 1mtr, 2dc, 2mtr, ch2, skip 1 st, [1mtr, 3dc] 3 times, 1mtr; rep from * to last 4 sts, ch4, skip 3 sts, 1dc, turn.

Row 30: Ch1, 1dc, ch4, skip 4ch-sp, 13dc, *ch2, skip 2ch-sp, 13dc; rep from * to last 4 sts, ch4, skip 4ch-sp, 1dc, cc, turn.

Row 31: Ch1, 1dc, 3mtr, ch3, skip 2 sts, 4dc, ch2, skip 1 st, 4dc, ch3, skip 2 sts, *1mtr, ch3, skip 2 sts, 2dc, ch2, skip 1 st, 3dc, ch2, skip 1 st, 2dc, ch3, skip 2 sts, 1mtr, ch3, skip 2 sts, 4dc, ch2, skip 1 st, 4dc, ch3, skip 2 sts; rep from * to last 4 sts, 3mtr, 1dc, turn.

Row 32: Ch1, 4dc, ch3, skip 3ch-sp, 4dc, ch2, skip 2ch-sp, 4dc, ch3, skip 3ch-sp, *1dc, ch3, skip 3ch-sp, 2dc, ch2, skip 2ch-sp, 3dc, ch2, skip 2ch-sp, 2dc, ch3, skip 3ch-sp, 1dc, ch3, skip 3ch-sp, 4dc, ch2, skip 2ch-sp, 4dc, ch3, skip 3ch-sp; rep from * to last 4 sts, 4dc, cc, turn.

Row 33: Ch1, 1dc, ch4, skip 3 sts, 2mtr, ch5, skip 4 sts, 1mtr, ch5, skip 4 sts, 2mtr, *ch2, skip 1 st, 2mtr, ch3, skip 2 sts, 1mtr, ch4, skip 3 sts, 1mtr, ch3, skip 2 sts, 2mtr, ch2, skip 1 st, 2mtr, ch5, skip 4 sts, 1mtr, ch5, skip 4 sts, 2mtr; rep from * to last 4 sts, ch4, skip 3 sts, 1dc, turn.

Row 34: Ch1, 1dc, ch4, skip 4ch-sp, 2dc, ch5, skip 5ch-sp, 1dc, ch5, skip 5ch-sp, 2dc, *ch2, skip 2ch-sp, 2dc, ch3, skip 3ch-sp, 1dc, ch4, skip 4ch-sp, 1dc, ch3, skip 3ch-sp, 2dc, ch2, skip 2ch-sp, 2dc, ch5, skip 5ch-sp, 1dc, ch5, skip 5ch-sp, 2dc; rep from * to last 4 sts, ch4, skip 4ch-sp, 1dc, cc, turn.

Row 35: Ch1, 1dc, 3mtr, ch3, skip 2 sts, 4mtr, ch2, skip 1 st, 4mtr, ch3, skip 2 sts, *1mtr, ch3, skip 2 sts, 2mtr, ch2, skip 1 st, 3mtr, ch2, skip 1 st, 2mtr, ch3, skip 2 sts, 1mtr, ch3, skip 2 sts, 4mtr, ch2, skip 1 st, 4mtr, ch3, skip 2 sts; rep from * to last 4 sts, 3mtr, 1dc, turn.

Row 36: Ch1, 4dc, ch3, skip 3ch-sp, 4dc, ch2, skip 2ch-sp, 4dc, ch3, skip 3ch-sp, *1dc, ch3, skip 3ch-sp, 2dc, ch2, skip 2ch-sp, 3dc, ch2, skip 2ch-sp, 2dc, ch3, skip 3ch-sp, 1dc, ch3, skip 3ch-sp, 4dc, ch2, skip 2ch-sp, 4dc, ch3, skip 3ch-sp; rep from * to last 4 sts, 4dc, cc, turn.

Row 37: Ch1, 1dc, ch4, skip 3 sts, 2mtr, 4dc, 1mtr, 4dc, 2mtr, *ch2, skip 1 st, 2mtr, 2dc, 1mtr, 3dc, 1mtr, 2dc, 2mtr, ch2, skip 1 st, 2mtr, 4dc, 1mtr, 4dc, 2mtr; rep from * to last 4 sts, ch4, skip 3 sts, 1dc, turn.

Row 38: Ch1, 1dc, ch4, skip 4ch-sp, 13dc, *ch2, skip 2ch-sp, 13dc; rep from * to last 4 sts, ch4, skip 4ch-sp, 1dc, cc, turn.

Row 39: Ch1, 1dc, 3mtr, *1dc, ch4, skip 3 sts, 5dc, ch4, skip 3 sts, 1dc, 1mtr; rep from * to last 3 sts, 2mtr, 1dc, turn.

Row 40: Ch1, 5dc, *ch4, skip 4ch-sp, 5dc, ch4, skip 4ch-sp, 3dc; rep from * to last 2 sts, 2dc, cc, turn.

Row 41: Ch1, 1dc, ch5, skip 4 sts, 3mtr, ch6, skip 5 sts, 3mtr, *ch4, skip 3 sts, 3mtr, ch6, skip 5 sts, 3mtr; rep from * to last 5 sts, ch5, skip 4 sts, 1dc, turn.

Row 42: Ch1, 1dc, ch5, skip 5ch-sp, 3dc, ch6, skip 6ch-sp, 3dc, *ch4, skip 4ch-sp, 3dc, ch6, skip 6ch-sp, 3dc; rep from * to last 5 sts, ch5, skip 5ch-sp, 1dc, cc, turn.

Row 43: Ch1, 1dc, 4mtr, *1dc, ch3, skip 2 sts, 5mtr, ch3, skip 2 sts, 1dc, 3mtr; rep from * to last 2 sts, 1mtr, 1dc, turn.

Row 44: Ch1, 6dc, *ch3, skip 3ch-sp, 5dc; rep from * to last st, 1dc, cc, turn.

Row 45: Ch1, 1dc, ch6, skip 5 sts, 2mtr, 1dc, ch4, skip 3 sts, 1dc, 2mtr, ch6, skip 5 sts, *2mtr, 5dc, 2mtr, ch6, skip 5 sts, 2mtr, 1dc, ch4, skip 3 sts, 1dc, 2mtr, ch6, skip 5 sts; rep from * to last st, 1dc, turn.

Row 46: Ch1, 1dc, ch6, skip 6ch-sp, 3dc, ch4, skip 4ch-sp, 3dc, ch6, skip 6ch-sp, *9dc, ch6, skip 6ch-sp, 3dc, ch4, skip 4ch-sp, 3dc, ch6, skip 6ch-sp; rep from * to last st, 1dc, cc, turn.

Row 47: Ch1, 1dc, 5mtr, 1dc, ch3, skip 2 sts, 3mtr, ch3, skip 2 sts, 1dc, *5mtr, [1dc, ch4, skip 3 sts] twice, 1dc, 5mtr, 1dc, ch3, skip 2 sts, 3mtr, ch3, skip 2 sts, 1dc; rep from * to last 6 sts, 5mtr, 1dc, turn.

Row 48: Ch1, 7dc, ch3, skip 3ch-sp, 3dc, ch3, skip 3ch-sp, 7dc, *ch4, skip 4ch-sp, 1dc, ch4, skip 4ch-sp, 7dc, ch3, skip 3ch-sp, 3dc, ch3, skip 3ch-sp, 7dc; rep from * to end, cc, turn.

Row 49: Ch1, 1dc, ch7, skip 6 sts, 2mtr, 3dc, 2mtr, *ch8, skip 7 sts, 3mtr, 1dc, 3mtr, ch8, skip 7 sts, 2mtr, 3dc, 2mtr; rep from * to last 7 sts, ch7, skip 6 sts, 1dc, turn.

Row 50: Ch1, 1dc, ch7, skip 7ch-sp, 7dc, *ch8, skip 8ch-sp, 7dc; rep from * to last 7 sts, ch7, skip 7ch-sp, 1dc, cc, turn.

Row 51: Ch1, 1dc, 6mtr, 1dc, ch6, skip 5 sts, 1dc, *7mtr, 1dc, ch6, skip 5 sts, 1dc; rep from * to last 7 sts, 6mtr, 1dc, turn.

Row 52: Ch1, 8dc, ch6, skip 6ch-sp, *9dc, ch6, skip 6ch-sp; rep from * to last 8 sts, 8dc, cc, turn.

Row 53: Ch1, 1dc, ch8, skip 7 sts, 5mtr, *ch10, skip 9 sts, 5mtr; rep from * to last 8 sts, ch8, skip 7 sts, 1dc, turn.

Row 54: Ch1, 1dc, ch8, skip 8ch-sp, 5dc, *ch10, skip 10ch-sp, 5dc; rep from * to last 8 sts, ch8, skip 8ch-sp, 1dc, cc, turn.

Row 55: Ch1, 1dc, 7mtr, 1dc, ch4, skip 3 sts, 1dc, *9mtr, 1dc, ch4, skip 3 sts, 1dc; rep from * to last 8 sts, 7mtr, 1dc, turn.

Row 56: Ch1, 9dc, ch4, skip 4ch-sp, *11dc, ch4, skip 4ch-sp; rep from * to last 9 sts, 9dc, cc, turn.

Row 57: Ch1, 1dc, ch9, skip 8 sts, 3mtr, *ch12, skip 11 sts, 3mtr; rep from * to last 9 sts, ch9, skip 8 sts, 1dc, turn.

Row 58: Ch1, 1dc, ch9, skip 9ch-sp, 3dc, *ch12, skip 12ch-sp, 3dc; rep from * to last 9 sts, ch9, skip 9ch-sp, 1dc, cc, fasten off Yarn B, turn.

Row 59: Ch1, 1dc, 8mtr, 3dc, *11mtr, 3dc; rep from * to last 9 sts, 8mtr, 1dc, turn.

Row 60: Ch1, 1dc in each st to end, cc to C, turn.

Rows 61 to 284: Rep Rows 5 to 60 a further 4 times, changing from C to D to C to B in turn at end of each Row 60.

Rows 285 to 286: Using A, rep Row 60 twice more.

Fasten off and weave in ends.

EDGING

Round 1 (RS): Join E with a slst in top right hand st, ch1 (does not count as st throughout), (1dc, ch2, 1dc) in same st, 1dc in each st to last st on top edge, (1dc, ch2, 1dc) in last st, rotate work 90 degrees, 1dc in each of next three row ends, *skip next row end, 1dc in each of next four row ends; rep from * to end of long side, finishing on any st in rep, rotate work, (1dc, ch2, 1dc) in first st on bottom edge, 1dc in each st to last st on bottom edge, (1dc, ch2, 1dc) in last st, rotate work, 1dc in each of next three row ends, **skip next row end, 1dc in each of next four row ends; rep from ** to end of long side, finishing on any st in rep, slst to beg dc, turn.

Round 2 (WS): Ch1, *1dc in each st to 2ch-sp, (1dc, ch2, 1dc) in ch-sp; rep from * around to end, slst to beg dc.

Fasten off and weave in all ends.

KEY

A   B, C or D

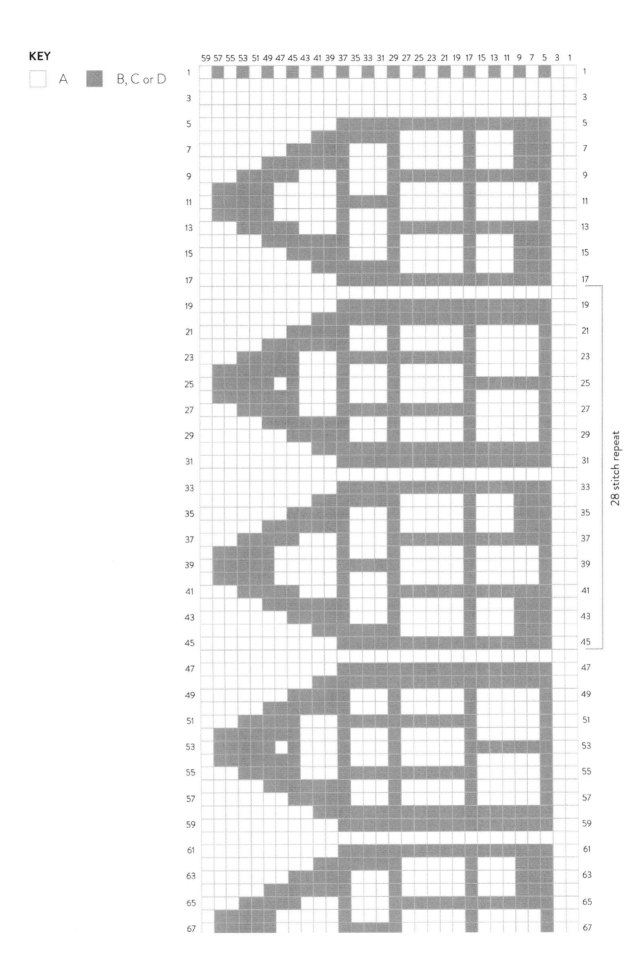

28 stitch repeat

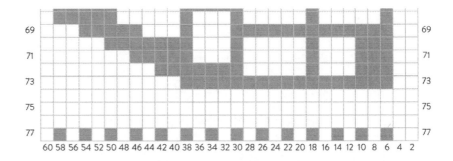

Each square represents a stitch.

To work from this chart, rotate it by 90 degrees clockwise. Read all odd-numbered (RS) rows from right to left, and all even-numbered (WS) rows from left to right.

Work rows 1 to 60 to start, and on subsequent repeats work rows 5 to 60.

TOP TIP

This would make a brilliant rug for a child's playroom in a soft, chunky yarn – perfect for make-believe games!

TOP TIP

A row of fringed tassels in E would look great if you want to add more detail to the edging.

Try a new colourway

BACKGROUND BEAUTY

Choose one of your favourite colours and let the background step forward into the limelight. A large expanse of a single colour can be breathtaking – this gorgeous forget-me-not blue is the star of the show in this design.

SPIN-OFF PROJECT:
Neon Street Wall Hanging

SKILL LEVEL:

This project is just begging to be customized… tassels AND pompoms maybe? How about a striped rainbow background? Sparkly hanging cord? I could have made so many of these but only one would fit in this book, so I went with neon. Because in my humble opinion you can never go wrong with a bit of perky-bright neon pink joy…

YOU WILL NEED

YARN

Scheepjes Colour Crafter (100% Acrylic), DK/light worsted, 100g (300m/328yds), in the following shades:

Pollare (2018); 1 ball (A)

Hilversum (1257); 1 ball (B)

Zandvoort (1218); 1 ball (C)

HOOK

4mm crochet hook

OTHER TOOLS AND MATERIALS

50cm (19¾in) length of wooden dowel, 12mm (½in) diameter

70cm (27½in) length of invisible thread

Tapestry needle

PATTERN MULTIPLES

Pattern works to a multiple of 28 stitches + 22 stitches for the starting chain.

TENSION (GAUGE)

20 sts and 24 rows measure 10 x 10cm (4 x 4in) over patt using a 4mm hook.

FINISHED SIZE

Main panel measures 42cm (16½in) wide x 28cm (11in) high after blocking, excluding hanging tabs and tassels

Wall hanging measures 42cm wide (16½in) x 41cm (16⅛in) high

Note

The main panel is made using A and B, then edged in C. After gentle blocking, hanging tabs are added along the top edge in C, and a row of tassels along the bottom edge in B. Finally, the wooden dowel is inserted into the tabs, and the invisible thread is attached.

INSTRUCTIONS

Main panel

Using A, ch78.

Row 1 (RS): 1dc in second ch from hook and in each ch to end, turn. (77 sts)

Rows 2 to 59: Now follow Dutch Houses Throw patt, starting at Row 2 (using A) and finishing at the end of Row 59, using A and B as indicated.

Rows 60 to 62: Using A, ch1, 1dc in each to end, turn.

Fasten off both yarns and weave in ends.

EDGING

Round 1 (RS): Join C with a slst in top right hand st, ch1 (does not count as st throughout), (1dc, ch2, 1dc) in same st, 1dc in each st to last st on top edge, (1dc, ch2, 1dc) in last st, rotate work 90 degrees, 1dc in each of next three row ends, *skip next row end, 1dc in each of next four row ends; rep from * to end of short side, finishing on any st in rep, rotate work, (1dc, ch2, 1dc) in first st on bottom edge, 1dc in each st to last st on bottom edge, (1dc, ch2, 1dc) in last st, rotate work, 1dc in each of next three row ends, **skip next row end, 1dc in each of next four row ends; rep from ** to end of short side, finishing on any st in rep, slst to beg dc, turn.

Round 2 (WS): Ch1, *1dc in each st to 2ch-sp, (1dc, ch2, 1dc) in ch-sp; rep from * around to end, slst to beg dc, turn.

Round 3 (RS): Ch1, *1dc in each st to 2ch-sp, (1dc, ch2, 1dc) in ch-sp; rep from * around to last side, 1dc in each st to end, slst to beg dc.

Fasten off and weave in ends.

Block main panel gently to pull it into a perfect rectangular shape.

HANGING TABS
(make 6)

Work along top edge.

With RS facing, join C with a slst in 2ch-sp in top right-hand corner, leaving a long tail for sewing.

***Row 1 (RS):** Ch1 (does not count as st throughout), 1dc in same st as join, 1dc in each of next 7 sts, turn. (8 dc)

Rows 2 to 14: Ch1, 1dc in each st to end, turn. (8 dc)

Fasten off at end of Row 14, weave in final end.

Fold tab over onto WS and use long tail to whip stitch top edge of Row 14 to bottom edge of Row 1 to make a hanging tab.**

With RS facing, skip next 7 sts on top edge of Main Panel, join C with a slst in next st (leaving a long tail for sewing), rep from * to **.

Continue along top of main panel in this way, skipping 7 sts between each tab, making the final tab in last 8 sts (2ch-sp at top left-hand corner counts as final st).

Fasten off and weave in all ends.

Push the dowel through the hanging tabs. Tie the invisible thread to each end of the wooden dowel, and then tuck the loose end of the thread under the hanging tab at each end to hide it.

TASSEL FRINGE

(make 41)

Cut four 25cm (9¾in) lengths of B, hold them together and fold them in half. Poke the looped end through the first st in the bottom left-hand corner of the main panel (thread them onto a tapestry needle to insert through the st if this is easier). Take the cut ends of yarn and thread them through the loop, then pull them all the way through to finish. Rep every 2 sts along bottom edge. Trim to neaten up.

TOP TIP

This project would make a fabulous house-warming gift.

Yes Throw

SKILL LEVEL:

An explosion of positivity and colour! YES is the perfect word to turn into crochet – such a concise, neat little word but it says so much. I am so grateful to our amazing worldwide community of crafters and makers: it's a welcoming, encouraging, inspiring and incredibly positive place to be, and I love it here. YES is a design that celebrates all of this! I believe we are better people when we are making stuff and connecting with each other. And we might as well throw some mad colour-love into the mix while we're at it.

YOU WILL NEED

YARN

Scheepjes Colour Crafter (100% Acrylic), DK/light worsted, 100g (300m/328yd), in the following shades:

Zandvoort (1218); 4 balls (A)

Hilversum (1257); 1 ball (B)

Drachten (1827); 1 ball (C)

Pollare (2018); 2 balls (D)

Nijmegen (1712); 1 ball (E)

Leuven (2008); 1 ball (F)

HOOK

5.5mm hook

OTHER TOOLS

45mm (1¾in) pompom maker

PATTERN MULTIPLES

Pattern works to a multiple of 28 stitches + 4 stitches for the starting chain.

TENSION (GAUGE)

14 sts and 18 rows measure 10 x 10cm (4 x 4in) over patt using a 5.5mm hook.

FINISHED SIZE

Approx. 102 x 137cm (40¼ x 54in) excluding pompoms

Notes

Keep A attached throughout as the background colour. Eleven 'YES' sections are made in the following yarn sequence: B, C, D, E, F, D, B, C, D, E, F. Work the first YES section using A and B as indicated, then join each new colour in sequence for the start of Row 5 and fasten it off at the end of Row 22 for each subsequent repeat. No edging is added, so the little pops of colour are visible down the two long sides.

The 20 pompoms are made with B to F, 10 for each end. For the bottom edge, attach pompoms in the following sequence: D, E, F, D, B, C, D, E, F, D. For the top edge, attach them in the following sequence: D, B, C, D, E, F, D, B, C, D.

INSTRUCTIONS

Using A, ch144.

Row 1 (RS): 1dc in second ch from hook, and in each ch to end, turn. (143 sts)

Rows 2 to 4: Ch1 (does not count as st throughout), 1dc in each st to end, turn. Cc to B at end of Row 4.

Row 5: Ch1, 1dc, ch3, skip 2 sts, 7dc, ch2, skip 1 st, 7dc, ch5, skip 4 sts, 3dc, *ch7, skip 6 sts, 7dc, ch2, skip 1 st, 7dc, ch5, skip 4 sts, 3dc; rep from * to last 6 sts, ch6, skip 5 sts, 1dc, turn.

Row 6: Ch1, 1dc, ch6, skip 6ch-sp, 3dc, ch5, skip 5ch-sp, 7dc, ch2, skip 2ch-sp, 7dc, *ch7, skip 7ch-sp, 3dc, ch5, skip 5ch-sp, 7dc, ch2, skip 2ch-sp, 7dc; rep from * to last 3 sts, ch3, skip 3ch-sp, 1dc, cc to A, turn.

Row 7: Ch1, 1dc, 2mtr, ch4, skip 3 sts, 4dc, 1mtr, 4dc, ch4, skip 3 sts, 4mtr, ch4, skip 3 sts, *6mtr, ch4, skip 3 sts, 4dc, 1mtr, 4dc, ch4, skip 3 sts, 4mtr, ch4, skip 3 sts; rep from * to last 6 sts, 5mtr, 1dc, turn.

Row 8: Ch1, *6dc, ch4, skip 4ch-sp, 4dc, ch4, skip 4ch-sp, 9dc, ch4, skip 4ch-sp; rep from * to last 3 sts, 3dc, cc, turn.

Row 9: Ch1, 1dc, ch3, skip 2 sts, 3mtr, ch10, skip 9 sts, 3mtr, ch5, skip 4 sts, 3mtr, *ch7, skip 6 sts, 3mtr, ch10, skip 9 sts, 3mtr, ch5, skip 4 sts, 3mtr; rep from * to last 6 sts, ch6, skip 5 sts, 1dc, turn.

Row 10: Ch1, 1dc, ch6, skip 6ch-sp, 3dc, ch5, skip 5ch-sp, 3dc, ch10, skip 10ch-sp, 3dc, *ch7, skip 7ch-sp, 3dc, ch5, skip 5ch-sp, 3dc, ch10, skip 10ch-sp, 3dc; rep from * to last 3 sts, ch3, skip 3ch-sp, 1dc, cc, turn.

Row 11: Ch1, 1dc, 2mtr, ch4, skip 3 sts, 9mtr, ch4, skip 3 sts, 4mtr, ch4, skip 3 sts, *6mtr, ch4, skip 3 sts, 9mtr, ch4, skip 3 sts, 4mtr, ch4, skip 3 sts; rep from * to last 6 sts, 5mtr, 1dc, turn.

Row 12: Ch1, *6dc, ch4, skip 4ch-sp, 4dc, ch4, skip 4ch-sp, 9dc, ch4, skip 4ch-sp; rep from * to last 3 sts, 3dc, cc, turn.

Row 13: Ch1, 1dc, ch3, skip 2 sts, 3mtr, 4dc, ch2, skip 1 st, 4dc, 3mtr, ch2, skip 1 st, 3dc, 3mtr, 3dc, *ch4, skip 3 sts, 3mtr, 4dc, ch2, skip 1 st, 4dc, 3mtr, ch2, skip 1 st, 3dc, 3mtr, 3dc; rep from * to last 3 sts, ch3, skip 2 sts, 1dc, turn.

Row 14: Ch1, 1dc, ch3, skip 3ch-sp, 9dc, [ch2, skip 2ch-sp, 7dc] twice, *ch4, skip 4ch-sp, 9dc, [ch2, skip 2ch-sp, 7dc] twice; rep from * to last 3 sts, ch3, skip 3ch-sp, 1dc, cc, turn.

Row 15: Ch1, 1dc, 2mtr, 4dc, ch4, skip 3 sts, 1mtr, 4dc, ch4, skip 3 sts, 1mtr, ch4, skip 3 sts, 3dc, ch4, skip 3 sts, *3mtr, 4dc, ch4, skip 3 sts, 1mtr, 4dc, ch4, skip 3 sts, 1mtr, ch4, skip 3 sts, 3dc, ch4, skip 3 sts; rep from * to last 3 sts, 2mtr, 1dc, turn.

Row 16: Ch1, *[3dc, ch4, skip 4ch-sp] twice, 1dc, ch4, skip 4ch-sp, 5dc, ch4, skip 4ch-sp, 4dc; rep from * to last 3 sts, 3dc, cc, turn.

Row 17: Ch1, 1dc, ch7, skip 6 sts, 3mtr, ch6, skip 5 sts, 3mtr, ch2, skip 1 st, 3mtr, ch4, skip 3 sts, 3mtr, *ch8, skip 7 sts, 3mtr, ch6, skip 5 sts, 3mtr, ch2, skip 1 st, 3mtr, ch4, skip 3 sts, 3mtr; rep from * to last 3 sts, ch3, skip 2 sts, 1dc, turn.

Row 18: Ch1, 1dc, ch3, skip 3ch-sp, 3dc, ch4, skip 4ch-sp, 3dc, ch2, skip 2ch-sp, 3dc, ch6, skip 6ch-sp, 3dc, *ch8, skip 8ch-sp, 3dc, ch4, skip 4ch-sp, 3dc, ch2, skip 2ch-sp, 3dc, ch6, skip 6ch-sp, 3dc; rep from * to last 7 sts, ch7, skip 7ch-sp, 1dc, cc, turn.

Row 19: Ch1, 1dc, 6mtr, ch4, skip 3 sts, 5mtr, ch4, skip 3 sts, 1mtr, ch4, skip 3 sts, 3mtr, ch4, skip 3 sts, *7mtr, ch4, skip 3 sts, 5mtr, ch4, skip 3 sts, 1mtr, ch4, skip 3 sts, 3mtr, ch4, skip 3 sts; rep from * to last 3 sts, 2mtr, 1dc, turn.

Row 20: Ch1, *[3dc, ch4, skip 4ch-sp] twice, 1dc, ch4, skip 4ch-sp, 5dc, ch4, skip 4ch-sp, 4dc; rep from * to last 3 sts, 3dc, cc, turn.

Row 21: Ch1, 1dc, ch3, skip 2 sts, [4dc, 3mtr, ch2, skip 1 st] twice, 3mtr, ch4, skip 3 sts, 3mtr, *ch4, skip 3 sts, [4dc, 3mtr, ch2, skip 1 st] twice, 3mtr, ch4, skip 3 sts, 3mtr; rep from * to last 3 sts, ch3, skip 2 sts, 1dc, turn.

Row 22: Ch1, 1dc, ch3, skip 3ch-sp, 3dc, ch4, skip 4ch-sp, 3dc, [ch2, skip 2ch-sp, 7dc] twice, *[ch4, skip 4ch-sp, 3dc] twice, [ch2, skip 2ch-sp, 7dc] twice; rep from * to last 3 sts, ch3, skip 3ch-sp, 1dc, cc, fasten off B, turn.

Row 23: Using A, ch1, 1dc, 2mtr, [7dc, 1mtr] twice, 3dc, 3mtr, 3dc, *3mtr, [7dc, 1mtr] twice, 3dc, 3mtr, 3dc; rep from * to last 3 sts, 2mtr, 1dc, turn.

Rows 24 to 26: Ch1, 1dc in each st to end, turn. Cc to C at end of Row 26, do not fasten off A.

Rows 27 to 246: Rep Rows 5 to 26 a further 10 times, following the yarn sequence in Notes.

Fasten off and weave in ends.

POMPOMS
(make 20)

Using the pompom maker, make three pompoms in each of B, C, E and F and eight in D. Trim to shape. Sew one to each corner of the Throw and space eight at regular intervals along each short end, referring to Notes for the colour sequence. Weave in all ends to finish.

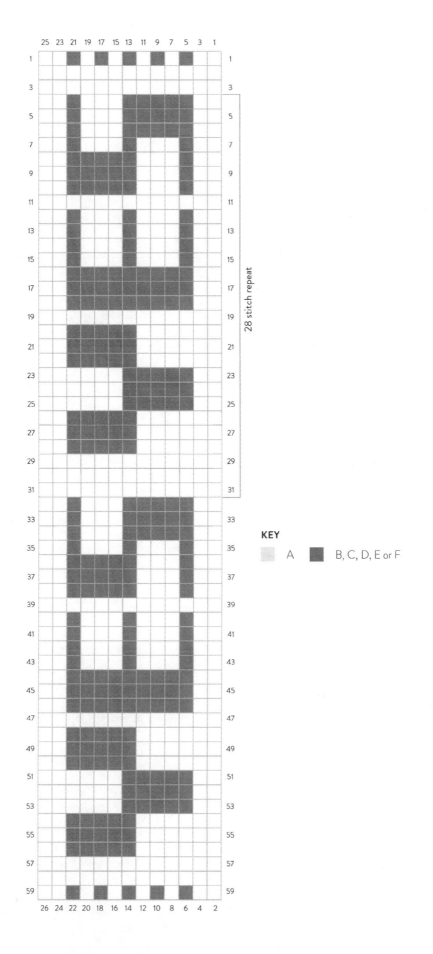

KEY

A   B, C, D, E or F

28 stitch repeat

Each square represents a stitch.

To work from this chart, rotate it by 90 degrees clockwise. Read all odd-numbered (RS) rows from right to left, and all even-numbered (WS) rows from left to right.

Work rows 1 to 26 to start, and on subsequent repeats work rows 5 to 26.

TOP TIP

This is not a symmetrical design – keep a close eye on the second row of each colour as it's the first row in reverse.

TOP TIP

This pattern is not symmetrical, so left-handed makers should follow the chart (working the rows in the opposite direction to that stated, so starting with Row

2 then Row 1, Row 4 then Row 3, and so on) instead of following the written instructions.

Try a new colourway

BUBBLEGUM TONES

Pastels aren't everyone's cup of tea, but you can definitely add a funky, modern spin by introducing slightly bolder bubblegum colours to this traditional palette. A splash of turquoise and bold lilac can add a touch of flamboyance and fun. Pretty but also punchy!

SPIN-OFF PROJECT:
Rebel Rainbow Tote

Clashy rainbow stripes and a big YES slogan: this tote is a little bit of a showstopper. I'll be honest, I'm not a natural shopper; I tend to grab it, pay for it, and get out as fast as possible. But I DO like a nice bag. Hence this tote, which has actually improved my shopping enthusiasm no end. When you catch yourself admiring the reflection of your bag in the supermarket window, then you know shopping just got more fun.

YOU WILL NEED

YARN

Scheepjes Linen Soft (27% linen/47% cotton/26% acrylic), DK/light worsted, 50g (135m/147yds), in the following shades:

Pale grey (618); 3 balls (A)

Teal (608); 1 ball (B)

Pink (626); 1 ball (C)

Yellow (631); 1 ball (D)

Dark blue (611); 1 ball (E)

Purple (625); 1 ball (F)

HOOK

3mm crochet hook

OTHER TOOLS AND MATERIALS

Approx. 1m (1yd) sturdy lining fabric

140cm (55in) strong grey webbing tape, 38mm (1½in) wide

Sewing needle, thread and pins

Sewing machine (optional)

Magnetic sew-on button (optional)

PATTERN MULTIPLES

Pattern works to a multiple of 28 stitches + 4 stitches for the starting chain.

TENSION (GAUGE)

19 sts and 24 rows measure 10 x 10cm over dc using a 3mm hook.

FINISHED SIZE

Panel measures approx. 42cm (16½in) wide x 41cm (16⅛in) high

Bag measures approx. 40cm (15¾in) wide x 39cm (15⅜in) high excluding handles

---

Note

The tote bag is made of two identical crocheted panels, worked from the bottom up. Once finished they are sewn together, and box corners are sewn into the bottom corners to add depth to the bag if required. Next, a fabric lining is made and inserted into the bag, the handles are placed between the lining and panels, then everything is stitched securely into place. A magnetic button is sewn on the inside if required.

INSTRUCTIONS

Panel

(make 2)

Using A, ch88.

Row 1 (RS): 1dc in second ch from hook and in each ch to end, turn. (87 dc)

Rows 2 to 26: Ch1 (does not count as st throughout), 1dc in each st to end, turn. Cc to C at end of Row 26, fasten off A.

Rows 27 to 50: Rep Row 2, working 6 rows in C, 6 rows in D, 6 rows in E, 6 rows in F. Cc to A at end of Row 50, fasten off F.

Rows 51 to 54: Ch1, 1dc in each st to end, turn. Cc to B at end of Row 54.

Rows 55 to 76: Now follow YES Throw patt, starting at Row 5 (using B) and finishing at end of Row 26, using A and B as indicated.

Fasten off A and B at end of Row 76, cc to F.

Rows 77 to 100: Rep Row 2, working 6 rows in F, 6 rows in E, 6 rows in D, 6 rows in C. Cc to A at end of Row 100, fasten off C.

Rows 101 to 102: Ch1, 1dc in each st to end, turn.

Fasten off A, weave in all ends.

ASSEMBLY

Cut out two pieces of lining fabric to the same width as the panel, but add 2cm (¾in) to the height for the top seam. Put to one side.

Panels

Place the two crocheted panels RS together and tack or pin along the side and bottom edges. Either hand or machine sew around these three sides, with a 1cm (⅜in) seam allowance. Remove the tacking stitches or pins.

To add depth to the bag (if required), make box corners as follows: With WS facing out, pinch across a bottom corner to make a triangle, so the side seam sits directly on top of the bottom seam. With seams opened out to reduce bulk, sew a small straight line 3cm (1⅛in) from the tip of the triangle. Repeat of the other side. Sew the loose corners to the bottom edge of the bag to hold them in place. Turn the bag RS out.

Lining

Join the two pieces of lining fabric together as for the crocheted panels, including the box corners if necessary, using a 1.5cm (⅝in) seam so the lining will be slightly smaller than the bag. With WS still facing out, iron a 2cm (¾in) hem around the top edge onto the WS. Insert the lining into the bag, with RS showing inside the bag. The lining should sit just under the top edge so it is not visible on the outside. Pin or tack into place, leaving two gaps for the handles on each side.

Handles

Cut the webbing in half. Insert the ends of the webbing into the top seam of the bag by 2cm (¾in), between the crocheted panel and the lining, with one handle on each side. Sew around the top edge of the bag to secure everything together, including the handles.

Sew the magnetic button onto the top inside edge, if used.

TOP TIP

It's very easy to customize your tote: you can change the colours to suit your wardrobe, add more or fewer stripes of colour… make this one your own!

Basic crochet techniques

These are the basic crochet stitches that you will need; see Understanding Mosaic Crochet for details of how to work the treble as a mosaic treble (mtr).

SLIPKNOT

An essential knot in crochet which attaches the yarn to the hook.

Make a loop in the yarn about 15 cm (6 in) from the end. Insert the hook through the loop from front to back, grab the ball-end of the yarn and draw it through the loop to the front. (A)

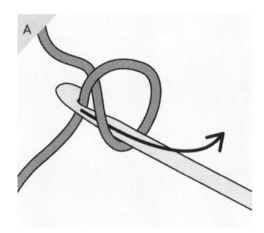

Pull both ends of the yarn to secure the knot around the hook. Do not pull too tightly, leave the slipknot slightly loose on the hook. (B)

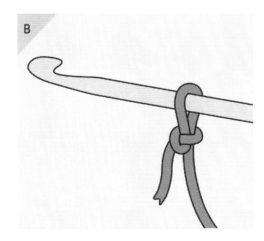

CHAIN STITCH (CH)

Many crochet projects start by making a length of chain.

With the yarn attached to the hook with a slipknot, hold the hook in your dominant hand, and the working yarn and the yarn end just under the hook in your other hand. Twist the hook around the back and under the working yarn (this is called 'yarn round hook' or 'yrh') and grab the yarn. (C)

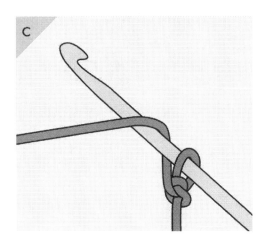

Use the hook to pull the yarn loosely through the slipknot to the front. The first chain stitch is complete. Repeat this 'twist, yrh and pull through' technique to form a length of chain. (D)

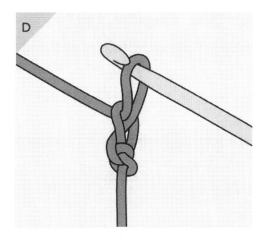

DOUBLE CROCHET (DC)

A small, dense stitch which forms the basis of mosaic crochet.

Insert the hook into the stitch from front to back, yarn round hook (yrh), pull the yarn through the stitch to the front. (E)

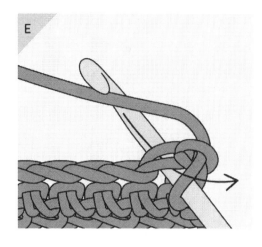

There will now be two loops on the hook, yrh again. (F)

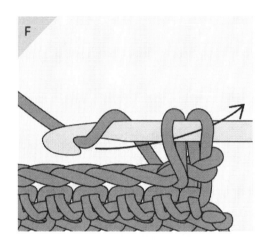

Pull the yarn through both loops on the hook to finish the stitch. (G)

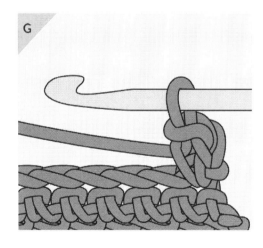

TOP TIP

When working your crochet stitches, make sure you always insert the hook through both loops of the stitch in step 1.

DOUBLE CROCHET TWO STITCHES TOGETHER (DC2TOG)
A stitch that is used to decrease two stitches into one stitch.

Insert the hook in the first stitch from front to back, yarn round hook (yrh), pull the yarn through the stitch to the front (there will be two loops on the hook). (H)

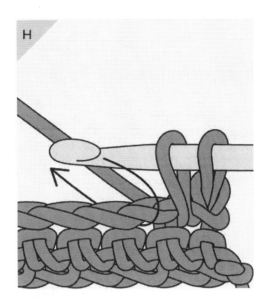

Insert hook in the next stitch, yrh, pull the yarn through the stitch (there will be three loops on the hook), yrh, pull the yarn through all three loops on the hook to finish the stitch. (I)

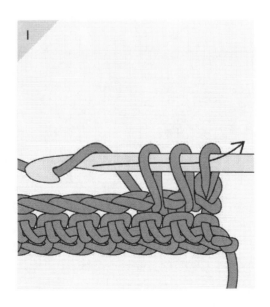

HALF TREBLE CROCHET (HTR)

A slightly taller stitch than a double crochet.

Yarn round hook (yrh), insert hook into the stitch from front to back. (J)

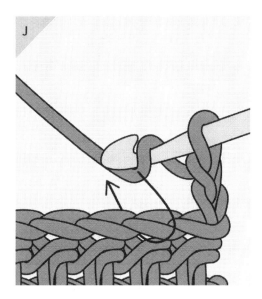

Yrh and pull the yarn through the stitch to the front (there will be three loops on the hook). (K)

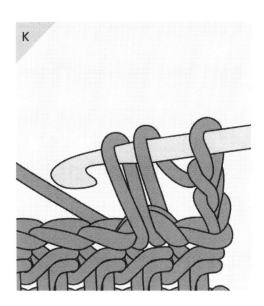

Yrh, pull the yarn through all three loops on the hook to finish the stitch. (L)

SLIP STITCH (SLST)

A stitch with no height, useful for joining one stitch to another.

Insert the hook into the stitch from front to back, yarn round hook. (M)

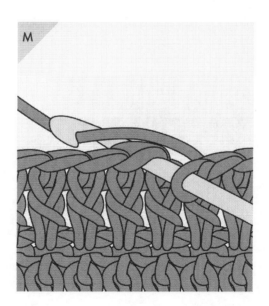

Pull the yarn through the stitch and through the loop on the hook to finish the stitch. (N)

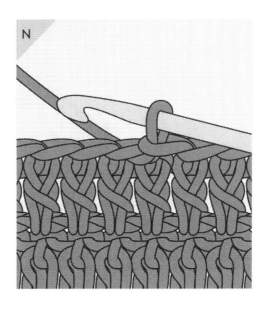

TREBLE CROCHET (TR)

A longer stitch, essential for mosaic crochet.

Yarn round hook (yrh), insert hook into the stitch from front to back. (O)

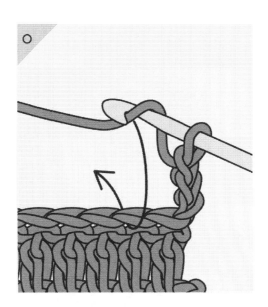

Yrh and pull the yarn through the stitch to the front (there will now be three loops on the hook). (P)

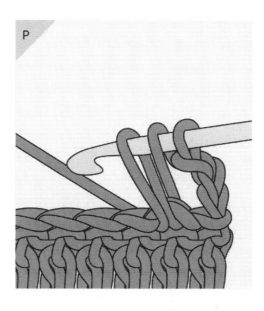

Yrh, pull the yarn through the first two loops on the hook (there will be two loops on the hook). (Q)

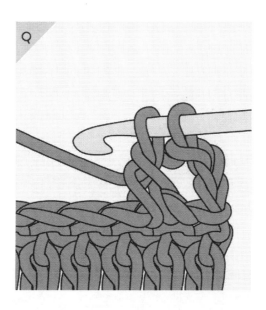

Yrh, pull the yarn through the remaining two loops on the hook to finish the stitch. (R)

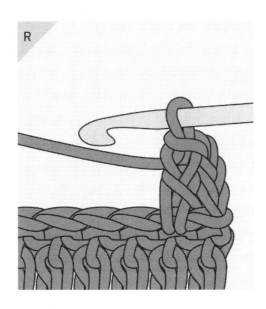

HOW TO MAKE A POMPOM

To make pompoms without a pompom maker, cut two circles of card to the same diameter as your pompom, then cut a second hole out of the centre of each. Place the two circles together and wind the yarn all the way around them in the same way. (S)

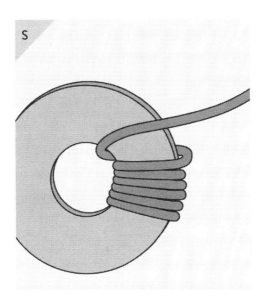

Easing the point of the scissors between the layers, cut through all the yarn around the edge. (T)

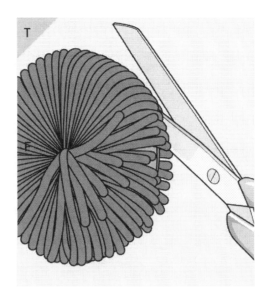

Tie a length of yarn around the centre of the pompom, pulling it very tight, and knot it securely several times before removing the pompom maker or card. (U)

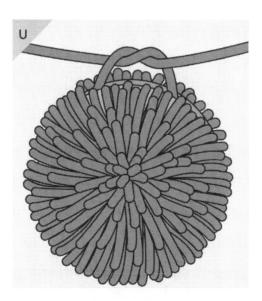

TOP TIP

If you are using a pompom maker, wind the yarn around each half until it is plump and padded, then push the two halves together. Finish as detailed above left.

Made in United States
Troutdale, OR
07/29/2024

21608527R10135